The Stories of Kulang Toat
A Legend in Africa's Nuer Land

Written by
Weirial Baluang

with illustrations by
Daud M. Boro

ISBN 978-0-6485028-4-5
© Weirial Baluang, 2019

Published by Africa World Books Pty. Ltd.
(www.africaworldbooks.com)

All rights reserved. No part of this publication may be reproduced, stored in a retrieval system, or transmitted, in any form, or by any means, electronic, mechanical, photocopying, recording or otherwise, without the prior permission of the publishers.

This book is sold subject to the conditions that it shall not, by way of trade or otherwise, be lent, re-sold, hired out or otherwise circulated without the publisher's prior consent in any form of binding or cover other than in which it is published and without a similar condition including the condition being imposed on the subsequent purchaser.

Design and typesetting: Africa World Books

Dedication

This book is dedicated to my father, the late Paul Gatyiel Puok, my mother, Mary Nyakume Gew Nyak (Komena) and my lovely grandmother, the late Mary Nyayiey Mut Nen (Nyadhuor), the best grandmother in the whole world.

About the Author

Weirial Baluang was born on 5th of May 1990 in Giil village, Leer, South Sudan. He is a novelist, reader, and teacher. He has taught English Literature in high school for years. He is best known for his first non-fiction novel, *The Stories of Kulang Toat, A Legend in Africa's Nuer Land*. *America Destroyed Me* is his second book. *Family Tears Apart* is Baluang's upcoming novel among other short stories for kids and adults including Grammar and Phonics books for beginners.

Table of Contents

	A Note to Readers	9
	A Note to the Nuer People	10
	A Note from the Publisher	10
	The Naath/Nuer tribe	11
	The Ten Sins of the Nuer	18
	Kulang Toat Kang	23
1	Kulang's Disgraceful Marriage	27
2	The Hoax over Cow's Milk	40
3	Kulang's Brother-in-Law is Killed	46
4	The Fight over Hippo's Legs	51
5	Kulang's Sarcasm	57
6	Kulang Burns the Walking Stick	53
7	Kulang Dismisses his Friend	68
8	Kulang Expels his Son	74
9	Kulang Apprehends Sugar	80
10	Kulang and the Four Feasts	89
11	Kulang Succumbs to Treachery	94
12	Kulang Suffers Revenge	98
13	Kulang Faces off with Anyanya Fighters	110
14	Kulang's Greed and Insanity	116
15	Kulang Discovers the Telephone	120
16	Kulang Denies his Nephew	124
17	Kulang and Food Security	128

18	The Visitor from Far	133
19	Kulang in the Forest of Dates	137
20	Kulang Declares Rebellion	142
21	Kulang Sues his Dog	146
22	Death Accusation	150
23	Kulang Finds his Like	154
24	The Cold War	157
25	Kulang Sells his Cattle	161
26	The Buttock Target	164
27	Kulang's Small-Scale Farming	167
28	The Young Men Regret	171
29	Kulang Interrupts the Soldiers	174
30	The Fight over Salt	177
31	Nyachom's Mother Regrets	180
32	Kulang Insults his Bride	183
33	Kulang in the Church	185
34	Kulang Insults the Head Chief	190
35	Kulang and Tut Kuach Diew	194
36	Kulang at the Marriage Ceremony	199
37	Kulang and the Deaf Man	203
38	Kulang Identifies his Likes	206
39	Kulang on Goalgoali Island	209
40	Kulang wants Nyachom Dead	212
41	Kulang Befriends a Trickster	215
42	Kulang Regrets Chasing Nyachom away	225
43	Kulang Chases away Nyachom's Sister	228
44	Kulang Rejects Ghost Marriage	230

45	Kulang Betrays his Family	235
46	Kulang's Broken Promise	239
47	Relocation inside the Hut	244
48	The Fight over the Grassland	246
49	The Lazy Neighbour	249
50	The Death of Kulang	253
51	The Death of Nyachom	258
	Teaching Resources	263
	A Glossary of Nuer Words and Phrases	280
	Acknowledgments	283

A Note to Readers

Kulang Toat Kang, (1896 – September 1, 1968), was a member of South Sudan's Nuer tribe and was a hard worker and comedian, who had differing economic theories and practices to those the Nuer tribe usually practiced. His people culturally share everything including marriage dowries irrespective of one's economic status. Nuer people sometimes describe him ruthlessly with no mention of his ideas on working hard and safeguarding individual wealth.

Except for the illustrations and the related fictional stories of animals and birds in this book, every story is true. This book is a collection of more than fifty stories of a man whose life was occupied by philosophy, wisdom, idiocy, prejudice and selfishness. The book will make you laugh, smile and think and gives us an important glimpse into the daily lives and attitudes of the Nuer tribe during the 1900s. These must read stories are told in a clear and simple diction suitable for young persons and adults. It must be remembered throughout that Kulang was a confrontational and antagonistic person who was known for fickleness. Most of the stories about him have rich moral lessons concerning just hard work and show us the consequences of being a problematic individual and what trouble that can cause for the individual, their family and their community.

We advise that you:
1. Do not tell your friends that they behave like Kulang.
2. Do not behave like Kulang yourself.
3. Do not insult Kulang within the Nuer community.

A Note to the Nuer People

If your village's, clan's, grandfather's, grandmother's or relative's name was misspelled or illustrated roughly, or coincided with the names mentioned in this book, the writer wishes to apologize and assure you that nothing of that kind has been intentional.

Weirial Gatyiel Puok Baluang
July 2019

A Note from the Publisher

The publisher wishes to acknowledge and thank Dr Douglas H. Johnson for his invaluable help and support for Africa World Books and its mission of preserving and promoting African cultural and literary traditions and history. Dr Johnson and fellow historians have been instrumental in ensuring that African people remain connected to their past and their identity. Africa World Books is proud to carry on this mission.

The Naath/Nuer Tribe

The Nuer people have an ancient name of 'Naath'. They also refer to themselves as 'Nei-Ti-Naath' which means the true or original human beings.

The name 'Nei-Ti-Naath came about because the Nuer believed that there were wild animals that could turn into human beings to feed on people. The Nuer referred to such carnivores as 'Leet'. Leet lived in the same environment with human beings. One of the men-beasts nicknamed himself Gatluak Manguel, around the 1900s. He was believed to be from outside the Nuer tribe.

Gatluak Manguel came and settled among the Nuer and started to eat from them. He could be seen as a human being but later when he wanted to eat people, he could turn into a carnivore to make him easily feed on human flesh. There was concrete evidence that corroborated this act among the people in the Gawaar, Dok and Lak lands.

Gatluak was allegedly captured by the English in 1926 and imprisoned in Malakal. He was later reported to have died in prison while trying to escape. Out of those human flesh-eaters, the Nuer people distinguish themselves as 'Nei-Ti-Naath' to separate themselves from the carnivores in form of humans.

The Nuer is one segment of the Nilotic ethnic groups found primarily in the Nile Valley in South Sudan and the Western Ethiopian region of Gambella. Around 1820-1860AD, some clans from the Nuer sections in Bentiu migrated to the eastern side of the Nile and occupied their current locations which are today known as the Greater Nasir (Upper Nile), Greater Akobo (Jonglei) and

Greater Fangak (Jonglei). This migration and assimilation resulted in the creation of the Nasir, Maiwut, Longichuk, Ulang, Fangak, Ayod, Akobo, Nyirol, and Uror Counties.

These places were inhabited by other tribes and most of them were either incorporated and assimilated into the Nuer tribe or chased away. After the assimilation, the language of the Nuer on the eastern side of the Nile slightly changed due to the assimilation of most of the tribes into their community.

Nowadays, the Nuer people speak the same language with variations as the accents differ across each section as well as each geographical area. The early migration of the Nuer across the Nile divided them into different sections as follows:

The Eastern Nuer

The Eastern Nuer people mainly live in the eastern part of the Upper Nile and Gambella region in Western Ethiopia. They are generally called 'Gaat-Kiiryow' with three subsections as follows: Gaat-Jaak, Gaat-Jiok, and Gaat-Guang.

The Central Nuer

The Central Nuer people generally live in the southern part of the Upper Nile. They are as follows: Lou-Nuer (Gaat-Borchar), Gawaar (Gaat-Kandei), Lak (Gaat-Geka), and Thiang (Gaat-Geka).

The Western Nuer

The Western Nuer people live generally in the Western Upper Nile. They are as follows: Bul (Gaat-Cholgeah), Jagei (Gaat-Geka), Dok

(Gaat-Gueah), Nyuong (Gaat-Gueah), Leek (Gaat-Nyalthiang), Haak (Gaat-Bakolkuoth), and Western Jikany/Jikany Chieng (Gaat-Kiirkaker).

All these Nuer/Naath sections trace their creation to Koat Lich, a Tamarind tree in present day Koch that belongs to Gaat-Geka. The Koat Lich is believed to be the place where the Nuer originated from and where the first woman gave birth to the sons and daughters of the present-day descendants of the Nuer.

The Nuer cultural variations and their folklore are the subject of this book. Kulang Toat Kang, whose words, ideas and actions are known all over the Nuer land is a foundation of this piece of work.

Lifestyle, norms and customs

Before diving deep into Nuer folktales using Kulang's wisdom (or lack thereof) and attitudes as an example, it's vital to say something about the Nuer social life in terms of norms and customs. Like most Nilotic people, the Nuer people are pastoralists whose livelihoods centered on cattle's rearing and seasonal farming.

As a result, their economical livelihood is centered on a pastoral lifestyle, and so are their folklores and norms, which are also important to their traditional lifestyle. For instance, the marriage transaction among the Nuer requires the payment of dowry in the form of cattle to the bride's family. This is a common practice which has existed for many generations. Ghost marriage (marrying on behalf of a dead relative) is very common all over the Naath land as a way of keeping alive the lineage of the deceased.

The Naath/Nuer people are known to be monotheistic as they pray and sacrifice to a single God (Deng-Taath) or God the creator. Deng-Taath is the name of the God who created Heaven, Earth and other worlds including the Underworld.

The Nuer believed that He is assisted by His earthly helpers known as 'Dayiemni'. Dayiemni are the humans who sing admirations to Deng-Taath to please Him. In addition, Deng-Taath possesses humans who are called Gok-Kuothni or the vessels of God. It is through these people that God is represented on Earth. Nuer people have smaller gods that are also active and solve some problems among the community. They are called Kuuth and most of them are magically conceived and their presence does not last long.

The Nuer people's tales have been oral tales that consist of animal, bird and human characters collaborating together. In these oral tales, animals and birds appear in clearly human situations and the language of communication is purely Nuer and there is no way to identify an animal except by their poor pronunciation of the Nuer language or their inhuman actions. These tales show a simplified form of human behaviour although they retain their animals and birds form. Their moral lessons teach the young ones how to punish evil and reward good deeds in this world which is full of both good and bad people. These stories are either told by the fireside or on the papyrus mats at night. Both grownups and young ones would take turns in order to tell their stories which they were told during the day by either the visitors or the neighbouring kids.

One of the heroes of the Nuer Tales is the 'Rel-geng or Wan' (Fox) which the Nuer believed to be the cleverest of all animals at home and away. Fox is always called 'Gat-geng' (Son of Geng) by the children to show respect because he makes them laugh with his cunning and rib-tickling especially when he at last, after divorcing his sister from five husbands, gave her to God in marriage.

Gat-geng's previous in-laws paid heavily the price by either eating the husbands or the kids which were the children of his dear sister. The first victim of his sister's husbands was the tortoise that he forced into a burning fire on a particular night when they were chatting. The sister was surprised to see only the shell of her kids' father who ended up in Gatgeng's stomach. God finally brought an end to his humiliating tricks by punishing him.

Once a story was created, it would be disseminated by the children at daytime until it reached the far end of the Nuer land and sometimes beyond to those who speak the Nuer language. The uniformity of the story would depend on the disseminators as there are good and bad story tellers. A good storyteller would tell it in a way that could attract the new listeners and even encourage them to disseminate it willingly.

One of the commonest folklore stories has it that at one point in time there was a direct connection between the people and the heavenly Kuoth, long ago, until a little bird cut the rope that was used by people to go and take their complaints to Him directly in heaven. And the cutting of that rope brought the face-to-face relationship between humans with God to an end.

There was also a myth about Jakar and Gawar who claimed to have directly descended from heaven and came down to the world as tourists using a rope which was later cut by another bird and that kept them from returning to their homes in heaven after they landed in Jiath village (currently in Leer). The two brothers, Gawar and Jakar, currently occupy Ayod and other parts of Nuer land. They still believe that their linages directly link to God unlike the other Nuer clans. They call themselves sons and daughters of God as you are reading this book: Jakar-Kuoth (Jakar, son of God) and Gawar-Kuoth (Gawar, son of God).

As the traditional Nuer world view is focused around cattle, men are frequently addressed by names that refer to the form and colour of their favourite oxen. Women take names from the cows they milk. For example, 'Majok' which is the colour of a bull with white and black stripes. This is also exemplified by the writer's name 'Weirial'. 'Wei' means kraal or cattle' area and 'rial' means black, white and grey stripes. To connect the two separate Nuer words, you will have the direct translation in English as: 'Cattle camp of different colours'. Gatyiel is derived from the name for the colour grey. Many Nuer names come from cattle and this is because of their association to the cattle.

The Nuer men are initiated on their foreheads with six marks known as 'Gaar'. This initiation prepares the transition of a person from childhood to adulthood. At this point, the initiated can have a right to marry and be treated like an adult irrespective of his age. He has the responsibility of protecting the society from any external aggression. His father will be in a position to hand him the responsibility to look after his cattle and consult him on certain important issues.

The other practices are the 'Bier' (round marks dotted or tattooing on the faces of young people). It used to be widely practiced by the

Nuer people but now it is diminishing slowly. This type of practice was used for decoration.

In the Nuer community, marriage binds families together and promotes communal relationships among people of different villages and linages. Marriage is organized in such a way that social bonding and societal well-being is a vital component for bringing different communities together. Respect is given a paramount consideration when one chooses a life partner in the form of a wife/husband.

The Nuer people consider children as economic assets—girls, in particular, are valued more than the boys because of their economic role in bringing income to the family. They are monetized in such a way that the dowries from their marriage bring income for the whole family. The more girls one has, the richer he will become. If a young man, after vetting the girl's family, applied for marriage, the girl's family would vet him back as to whether he comes from good and well-respected family as opposed to some families with unacceptable behaviour.

The Ten Sins of the Nuer

In line with the Naath/Nuer customary ways of life, certain behaviours are against the traditions. The Naath believe in the promotion of a societal welfare by sharing things equally as well as treating everyone with the same respect that they deserve. While they are not socialist by nature, the Naath promote and reward a good behaviour, which promotes unity in the diversity of their tribe. The following comportments are prohibited in the Naath tribe:

Gluttony

Nuer people have a culture of food sharing in the times of scarcity and prosperity. They share equally every little thing they have. A person who does not share what he/she gets with others is considered greedy/selfish. No man/girl would choose to marry or befriend a greedy/selfish person. A greedy man or family known to have that background is usually denounced and isolated in the community.

The Evil Eye

According to the Nuer, an evil eyed-person or '*peeth*' is believed to have the power of inflicting harm to people he/she had a crush on. Once one is found to be an evil eye figure, he/she will be at risk of losing his/her lover before entering into marriage. '*Peeth*' is not even accepted in a normal relationship let alone marriage.

Slandering

Nuer people do condemn slandering seriously. It's a shame and embarrassment to be found a slanderer or lie-teller. Families known to have such character are discriminated and deprived of concluding marriage contract in the surrounding villages unless they migrate to become new people in a strange land so that no one would know about their maligning background.

Gossiping

A person known for practicing gossip is normally sanctioned by Nuer people. He/she could not even participate in the conversation/dialogue known to be confidential. A gossiper is sometimes called '*Nyabuobkah*' a name given to a small MSF plane which used to rotate between Nuer land and Kenya during the then Sudan's civil war of 20th century. The plane was believed to be a gossiper taking and bringing information heatedly.

Laziness

An individual who is bodily and mentally fit and healthy but sits idly without working, is considered '*Kaway*' which literally means 'Whiteman'. A person found to be Kaway is not allowed to conclude marriage by bride's or groom's family because their son/daughter could lead an unhappy life in groom's/bride's home. Laziness is what made Kulang Toat end relationships with many people.

Theft

Stealing is considered deviant by Nuer custom; a man/girl known for stealing in the community could never have a dating mate. The whole community gets embarrassed by a person having such character. A thief is believed to have a stealing fingernail by the Nuer which let him abandon theft only when it is cut.

Trouble-making

A person known to have a habit of causing difficulties, distress, worry or any kind of problem to people or making it possible for a conflict to arise and doesn't participate in it, is sanctioned. A groom is rejected by bride's family if their genetic factor had this habit.

Intoxication

Intoxication is not encouraged in Nuer society though most rites encompass the preparation and consumption of wine. Being physically and mentally controlled by the effects of alcohol or drugs is a shame in Nuer culture. A person is required to adjust his drinking habit to the extent that he maintains his rational mind clean and fit for standard thinking. Members of a family known to have intoxicating background find it difficult to win approval of the bride/groom's family if they happen to offer a marriage proposal.

Weakness

A person found to fear or lack confidence and courageousness during wars or any given fight is not accepted even in his home area. Nuer people like a courageous man to defend his household and community from all threats, be it human or animal attack. The Nuer people hate to death a person who is not brave, who is easily frightened, or tries to avoid danger or difficulties. Such a person is isolated completely. A coward is detected by the Nuer from the way he walks, speaks or even from his eyes.

Premarital sex/lust

Premarital sex is not only condemned by the Nuer alone but also in Christianity. The Holy Bible describes lust as sinful, a form of faithlessness and immorality that comes not from the father but from the world. Believers are warned to guard against it. The Nuer society doesn't encourage lust or sex before marriage at every turn. The virginity of a girl is praised and valued as it is always seen as sign of respect and quality for the girl.

The People In This Book

Kulang Toat

Nyachom Loang

Kulang's friend, Dhuorwia (Arab)

Chamkuán

Kulang's friend, Ruai Pab

Machar Tot

Bilbor

Nhial Puot

Golongpin

Gatkuoth Ruei Wuor

Kulang Toat Kang

Kulang Toat Kang was born to a Thiang-Nuer father and a Dok-Nuer mother, Nyadoak Kier, in 1896, at Toch village, in Fangak area. He was an African traditionalist from the South Sudanese tribe of Nuer in what was Sudan's former Southern region, which is now the Republic of South Sudan. Kulang belonged to the Chieng-Nyaleni sub-clan in Chieng-Geng in the Thiäng section of the Central Nuer.

Like many Nuer folktales, most folktales about Kulang have been passed on via oral traditions from one generation to another. Similar to anyone else, Kulang had a rough life, with both bad and good deeds, which shaped and cemented his world view, character, and wisdom.

During Kulang's lifetime, most of his fellow villagers viewed him as a selfish person but the fact is that he was an economist, philosopher, emotional speaker as well as an intelligent entertainer with a sharp tongue that had life and death powers. He sometimes behaved as if the whole world belonged to him or he saw it from another angle. Except for his journey to Dongola and when he was jailed in Fangak, he had never in his life slept in someone else's home or outside his home or even wanted to.

Kulang was known for flattering his wife Nyachom, who could read his thoughts and who could understand his parables and body language perfectly. He used to give her different virtuous names when she was preparing his food as he was known to have a serious appetite. He was a man of few words who valued hard work and always gave people hard times when they crossed his path. The stories about him have dominated Nuer traditional oral folklore since his death.

Kulang had few friends, one of whom was a guy, Ruai Pab, whom he had once accused and chased for allegedly telling a lie on the status or location of the moon on a given night.

He was a strong and generous man who helped other people in group cultivation work in his village in times of need. He always planted seeds in the gardens of the village's lazy people with or without their consent so that he would not be disturbed when harvesting commenced.

Kulang was a hard worker though he was often selfish and would not share what he had with others at all cost. He believed that without hard work, he would not get all the food he needed. He personally believed in self-reliance and valued those who worked for themselves but this often made him less than generous to those who genuinely needed his help. There are many stories about him that will live on for years among the Naath people and even beyond.

Kulang married his caring wife, Nyachom, who turned to be one of the strongest women of the time, under very dubious circumstances and treachery when he divorced his fiancée, Nyalora, whom he had first become engaged to. He later changed his mind on marrying her and instead married her little sister, Nyachom, for reasons related to food.

After marrying the little sister of his fiancée, Kulang and Nyachom had kids who were given funny Nuer names (all the names related to eating or cursing other people, etc.). For instance, the first name of his elder son was 'Chamkuan' which literally means 'Eat Food'. His younger son, Duer, means 'Evil'. He also gave funny names to his two dogs. For instance, the name of his first dog was 'Ken-Thiäng-dak', which meant, 'The Thiang clan didn't fall apart or break down'. And he named his second dog '*Guichi-Ha-Ngu*' which can be translated as 'Why are you looking at me?' Kulang's family and friends paid dearly for his appetite and his attitudes during his life.

It's no secret that his behaviour reflects his world view regarding self-reliance as a way of promoting an independent living in his community whose culture is sharing things together regardless of one's economic status. He always condemned lazy people and praised hardworking people who did not request anything from anybody. Kulang was not an admirer of the socialist ideology of sharing resources as well as supporting lazy people as part of the community policy.

He believed in hard work and trained people to have the same work ethic in not relying on others. He always appeared in different moods. Sometimes he appeared with a good idea and at other times he was ruthless. Most of his words related to self-reliance as he was a supporter of independent living. He would fit well in a capitalist world where everyone fends for themselves but a capitalist world is built on inequality between groups of people. He did not want to be burdened by those who could support themselves but chose to be lazy instead but he often failed to take into account those who genuinely needed his help.

In his lifetime, he was a man of few words, but the stories about him echoed all over the Naath land and beyond. Although there were some disappeared Nuer figures that were hardworking like Kulang, the stories about him never faded away after his death in 1968 as he was a man who considered sleep a waste of time. Farming was his favourite main pastime.

ONE

Kulang's Disgraceful Marriage

One day, Kulang decided to get married. He went in the early morning to the *Luak* (a traditional Kraal or dwelling place for cattle) of the girl's father and proposed to marry his daughter Nyalora.

Knowing he was a hardworking man, Kulang was accepted right away by all the family members. He was so happy that he composed a song right then and there to show his happiness to the girl's family. Per Nuer customary marriage, a legal marital union is usually recognized through the exchange of bride-wealth in the form of cattle to be paid by the groom's family to the bride's family.

Kulang went back home happily with his friends after he was given the green light to officially marry his chosen future wife. Three months later in the winter season he returned to the girl's family. However, before he could reach the house, he found kids playing in close proximity to his in-laws' home. Among the kids was a young girl Nyachom who was Nyalora's younger sister. Kulang hid himself out of sight under a big nearby tree when he saw kids playing. Then he called out to Nyachom with a very low-slung voice: "Nyachom! Nyachom!"

Meanwhile the kids were frightened as they could not see the caller, so they ran away in fear. Only little Nyachom remained and he showed himself to her. Kulang decided to talk to the young lady, Nyachom to inform her about his situation. He told her that he had two issues and that he was not sure whether Nyachom was the right person to help him in such situations.

When Nyachom responded confidently that she would try to solve them if she knew what the issues were, Kulang went ahead and narrated the situations,

"Initially, I have been hungry for the past few days," he said. "and I would like to eat a big fish to satisfy my hunger. Additionally, I would like you to call for me Nyalora—my future wife-to-be,"

It was later confirmed that the reason why Kulang said he had been hungry and needed only fish was merely because he had seen his fiancée's mother carrying fish home on that day.

In resolving these two issues, Nyachom told Kulang to wait for her until she would come back from the house. Kulang enthusiastically managed to tolerate and endure the cold winter outside the house waiting for the food according to Nyachom's advice. When Nyachom reached home she found out that there was a fish brought by her mother. She decided to act on her own without telling any member of her family. She went back and advised Kulang to hide himself under a big tree in the neighbourhood. She told him to wait there until midnight because she was going to bring the fish there when her family members slept.

In the evening, the father of Nyalora and Nyachom, called his daughters for a brief meeting and told them to cook the big fish

She told him to wait there until midnight because she was going to bring the fish there when her family members slept.

because the next day his age-mates were going to visit in response to his invitation. From there, Nyachom and her two cousins and her elder sister Nyalora started doing as they were told by their father.

When they put the fish in the cooking pot, Nyalora and her two cousins began to take a nap. Nyachom told them to sleep as she would monitor the pot on the fire because they were napping. Suddenly the girls fell asleep. When she noticed that all the girls were sound asleep, she removed the fish from the cooking pot and put it in a large dish and brought her father's drinking pot, filled it with water and hurried towards Kulang and served him in his hiding place. After he ate the whole fish and became fully satisfied, Nyachom collected the leftover and went home secretly at night. Upon arrival, she scattered the leftovers around the kitchen area, broke the cooking pot, left the door open, and called on their dog so that the blame would be on it instead of her or her sisters, and finally went to bed thereafter.

In the early morning the family members were surprised by what had happened because the fish was nowhere to be seen and only the fish's bones were scattered everywhere in the family compound. Saddened by the event, the mother and her two sons took their weapons to kill the dog, but the father advised them not to do so, for it would bring shame to the family as this was against the Nuer culture. Both the angry mother and her sons forgave the dog after the father's advice.

To rectify the situation as a result of the loss of the fish, the father provided a sheep to be slaughtered as a substitute for the lost fish, for he had already invited his age-mates. At midday, the old man's friends came and ate the meal and dispersed thereafter.

A month or so later, Kulang returned to the house of his fiancée Nyalora, to continue with the marriage process. In approaching his in-laws' compound, he employed the same strategy of hiding himself under the same tree and called on the same young girl (Nyachom) who was among the children playing in the neighbourhood where Kulang was hiding. When Nyachom heard somebody's voice calling her, she went to check out who was calling her. It was her sister's fiancé, who appeared and thanked her for solving the previous problem. However, Kulang now had another problem and asked Nyachom again whether she could solve it as well. Nyachom said she would try if she knew the nature of the problem.

Now, Kulang narrated his other problems:

"I have been hungry since the last two-three days and I believe that only milk and butter will satisfy me," he said. "The second issue is somewhat easy and that is, I want you to call my fiancé Nyalora, so I can talk to her."

Nyachom again said she would try. She left to fulfill Kulang's two demands. She first informed Nyalora about Kulang's message. Nyalora went to see her fiancé, Kulang, right away and Kulang told her to inform her father and uncles to expect him in the family *Luak* the next morning for the marriage process to start.

Meanwhile in the evening hours, Nyachom, devised a way to solve Kulang's other request. She decided to milk the three cows and put the milk of these three cows in a big gourd in fulfillment of Kulang's other demand. When dusk approached, Nyachom took the milk, dish, and spoon to Kulang's place of hiding. When she reached where Kulang was, she sat down and served him. Kulang helped himself by eating and drinking the milk until he became extremely satisfied. After that, Nyachom returned back home.

Remember, Nyachom had done all of these in secret as nobody knew what was going on. It's against the Nuer culture for an in-law to eat food or even drink water at his in-laws' place before the finalization of the marriage. When Nyachom reached home, she continued with her strategy of protecting herself from being blamed by her family members. She went ahead and broke the gourd, called upon their dog in pretense that the dog would be responsible for breaking such a big gourd. While the dog was eating up the gourd, Nyachom secretly left. When her sisters found the dog, Nyachom immediately called her brothers and father to come and see what had happened.

But her father asked the girls as to why they were crying.

"Your gourd was eaten up by the dog," said Nyachom sadly, with crocodile tears running down from her face as if she was badly hurt.

At that moment, her brothers hurried and tried to kill the dog again, but their father came to the defense of the dog and advised them not to do so as killing the dog would bring shame to the family. The young men listened to their father's advice and put down all their weapons at once.

At dawn the following morning, all male relatives and the father of Nyalora went to the *Luak* as custom demands, in order to wait for their bridegroom and his family members. To their astonishment, Kulang came alone and sat at the other side of the Luak which was traditionally supposed to be for in-laws. Per Nuer custom, seating is usually arranged in such a way that one side of the Luak is always reserved for the groom's family members and the other side usually belongs to the girl's family in the marriage negotiation.

The marriage always brings the two (Bride and groom) family members together. It was one of the reasons why the girl's family was surprised to see only Kulang, without his other family members to accompany him. When Kulang sat on his side of the *Luak*, he cleared his voice and announced the object of his visit.

"I have something to tell you my in-laws," he began to speak courageously. "Dear parents of Nyalora, allow me to say this. I actually mistook Nyachom's name for Nyalora's name at the very beginning. For that reason, I have now come to pronounce the name well by separating with one side of the *Luak* and marrying with the other side of it."

The marriage negotiation among the Nuer is usually very interesting as it's where proverbs are used when one is communicating. One doesn't go deeply to the point even when talking to a weak or cowardly person. That was why Kulang didn't directly go to the point by mentioning the girls' names but instead he said it in a parable by mentioning *Luak*'s sides.

The father of the girls who well understood Kulang's message replied, "It can't happen that you can partially divorce your fiancée and marry her little sister. This would mean that our marriage has come to an end." Immediately, the girls' uncle intervened and silenced the rest of the angry family members as he wanted to clarify from Kulang as to why he had changed his mind on marrying Nyalora, and instead decided to marry the younger sister, Nyachom.

"My son, Kulang," said the girls' uncle confidently. "What do you mean by the words that you have just spoken?"

"I am done with your daughter, Nyalora, and I have now decided to marry her younger sister, Nyachom," was Kulang's response.

When the father of the girls heard that, he yelled with a song and declared the end of Kulang's marriage as this was against the tradition and it was an insult to the family. The girls' uncle again stopped his brother and told him that, he was the one to answer Kulang's new proposal.

"My son, Kulang, has this reached the bottom of your heart to marry Nyachom?" asked the girls' uncle.

"Definitely, it's from below the bottom of my heart." Kulang simply replied.

Then the uncle tasked to be in charge of the marriage negotiation sent someone to go and call the two young ladies Nyalora and Nyachom to come and hear what Kulang had decided. When the two girls reached inside the *Luak* where the marriage was being discussed by their father, uncles, and relatives with Nyalora's fiancé Kulang, they sat down. As the two sisters sat, Kulang was busy surveying Nyachom's young body with skillful eyes as if to assure himself that she was attractive and ready to cook enough food at any time.

Their uncle told them that all things were usually good when decided by the people with their free will.

"Nyachom! Kulang wants to marry you, will you accept that?" asked the girls' uncle.

That very tough question made Nyachom's body become cold for a few minutes because all eyes and ears were turned to her and she was only a teenager. She now had no choice but to be brave enough to speak her mind.

"If you have accepted him then let him marry me, for I have no objection." Nyachom declared with eyes turned down, drawing things on the ground with all her fingers to reduce shyness. When Kulang heard Nyachom's decision, he jumped to his feet and danced happily and tried to make a traditional dance with whoever came to his sight from his in-laws.

Kulang was then told that the girl was underage, and for that reason, he had to wait for the girl to reach maturity.

But Kulang replied, "I will unquestionably wait even if it means waiting for fifty years."

On hearing this, all the participants laughed loudly at Kulang's reply.

In the end, Kulang went back happily as he had done something unthinkable, even to himself. This was one of the reasons why he had come to his marriage negotiation alone as his relatives would have discouraged him from doing something like that.

During the autumn season, Kulang came back with eight cattle to his in-laws and he was accepted by Nyachom and the family members.

———

A superstition story is told of a very beautiful hen. Her parents were very poor, so it was decided that whoever was able to afford her ridiculously high bride- price would be her groom. News of her beauty spread across all lands and soon it got to a great hawk prince. The prince decided to see for himself so he sneaked into the hen's village unnoticed.

When the hawk prince finally saw the hen he was enchanted at once just like someone who saw or greeted Nyariek Thing Luoy, the only 20th century most beautiful girl in Nuer-Land who was cursed and had also died unmarried for having the beauty beyond description. The Nuer elders said, whenever Nyariek looked at some youth, they would burst in a fight among themselves each claiming to have been the one who was looked by her. They also say that whenever she shook hand with a boy; the boy would spend the whole day with his palm-hand in his mouth.

The prince decided that no one would have the hen. This chicken was to be his only bride. The prince came with his family as custom demands. They paid her bride-price but little did the hawk know the hen and a wretched cock were madly in love. The hawk took his bride to his kingdom leaving the poor cock heartbroken. Because to marry other person's lover is a suicide, the cock could love none other besides his beloved hen who was taken because he had no cattle or wealth. The cock sneaked into hawk's kingdom, one morning after the hawk had gone hunting. He began to crow beautifully with different styles as he used when he was in love with his beautiful hen. The hen was drawn back to the sound of his majestic voice and remembered their unforgettable old days when they used to enjoy together.

Finally, the old lovers reunited and made a decision to elope this time for good. They had to go far to the land inhabited by human beings so that no one would ever see them again. When the hawk prince returned, he found his wife was missing and also the footprints of the cock all around his chambers. The hawk prince was devastated.

He sent message to the hen's parents to return back his cattle as custom demanded but they could not as the cows had already been divided among the relatives. As a result, the prince reported the case to his father 'the hawk king' who was no lover of peace. All this while he had been ravaging lizard kingdoms but what he had always wanted was to destroy the proud chickens who thought they had the greatest voice and were the most graceful amongst birds.

The king sent messages to all the hawk colonies around the world and declared war on all the chickens. The war is still on to this day as you are reading about Kulang Toat. That is why the hawk takes some of small chicks and the hen would say, '*Kuoth, Kuoth Kunen*' which literally means: 'God, God see this.' That story is known all over the Nuer land and children learn it at a young age.

Kulang knew that Nyachom would make a good wife and meet the demands of his stomach and needs as per the examination he had made when he was in courtship with Nyachom's elder sister, Nyalora. He knew very well that, beauty fades away and the ability to serve well remains.

If Nyalora had done all that were done by Nyachom, Kulang wouldn't have divorced her and she would have been his wife instead. The best preparation for tomorrow is for people to do their best today at all cost like Kulang. It is not in Nuer culture for a girl to give her fiancé something to eat before the marriage consummated as Nyachom did for Kulang.

Kulang found it meaningless to worry about getting criticized. He didn't want to make an elopement because the marriage could be settled in court and the relationship would not go smoothly. Elopement is believed to be a short cut to marriage especially for someone who is not accepted by the family of the girl.

If this issue occurred, the suitor would be required to pay twenty five head of cattle to the parents of the girl not more than twenty four hours after the elopement to avoid consequences and sometimes it can cause a feud between the two families. After the twenty five cattle are paid immediately, the parties fix a day for the haggling and bargaining based on the girl's character. The number of cattle may go up to a hundred or beyond. A man is forced to pay more cows as if to completely buy the bride.

If the bride kills a person, the husband usually made to be responsible to handle all that a court may impose. And if the wife is killed, compensation is usually paid to her husband as well as when she is hurt. If a man killed his wife, he would simply add some heads of cattle to the bride wealth that he had already paid. That is why a woman is treated like an asset and not as a life partner because the husband has full control over her life according to Nuer law and customs. After paying what was required by Nyachom's family, Kulang had all the rights to her as per the Nuer custom of marriage.

If you have accepted him then let him marry me, for I have no objection.

TWO

The Hoax over Cow Milk

After some years of marriage, when Kulang was exhausted by the unceasing coming of visitors that he always blamed on Nyachom, he decided to punish her by bringing home a new wife.

Although Kulang failed to get satisfaction from his wife, Nyachom, she was very lucky to be the first wife because in Nuer culture, the first wife is always the senior woman and the most respected wife in the family. So, Kulang decided to get married again since having more wives is allowed in Nuer custom—a typical African traditional social custom.

The Nuer custom of marriage legalizes patriarchal polygamy, where it is a norm for a man to have more than one wife. However, it is forbidden for a woman to have more than one husband. The more wives the man has, the richer he is considered, especially, when most of the children are females. Female kids bring more cattle into the family as they are treated as assets. A great number of wives is a status symbol showing that a man is rich and strong because it demonstrates that he is able to support, defend and feed all of them. In Nuer culture, the men are the leaders dictating things in the family. For example, in the marriage ceremonies and other occasions, the women are usually found more towards the back, with the men at the front.

Kulang, according to the culture, was free to marry as many more wives as he wished to. The family of the girl he wanted to marry was from the Chieng-Gong-Kiy village, near Payat-Lak. His village bordered the village of the girl's family. When he proposed to the girl, he was automatically accepted by the girl's parents as well as all their relatives because he was a hard worker as Nuer people do not like lazy people.

For that reason, he said to his in-laws he would return in four days so that the marriage was to be haggled as custom demands. At the end of four days, the wedding negotiation started and Kulang brought with him four cows. Three of them were lactating cows with calves and one of them was a heifer.

When the traditional wedding finished, all the pots of wine were divided equally among the wedding guests on the bridegroom's and the bride's sides as required by the custom. There were pots of wine for the uncle's side, parents, friends, in-laws as well as everyone who attended the traditional wedding. When the gifting of wine was completed, Kulang had not been given any and he called his wife Nyachom and complained about what had happened.

"How is the world now?" he asked sadly. "It seems like it is upside down and downside up. I am very thirsty in this so-called wedding. Can you get me a pot of wine so that I relieve my thirst, Sister?"

Kulang silently looked down like someone whose father had just died. Nyachom knew that her husband, Kulang, was only really suffering from the sound of his voice by the way he was calling her his 'sister'.

Immediately, Nyachom left for their home and brought a very big pot full of wine and gave it to him. Kulang drank the wine and became drunk for the rest of the night. He became so heavily drunk that his eyes were red and fierce like the eyes of an antelope caught by a hunter alive in the bush. He even got up from the bed and tried to walk about but he would fall down like a toddler learning to walk because he was so weak that his legs could hardly carry him.

The following day, they negotiated the bride-price with sticks according to the Nuer custom of marriage. A few days later, Kulang heard that his heifer had given birth and had a lot of milk among all the cows and that the milk was stored in a big gourd in the compound of his in-laws. He then thought of how to get the milk back: "Now I must get back my cow which gives more milk."

After a few days, he came back to his in-laws and called an emergency meeting concerning their dogs. Kulang told them that the agenda of the meeting was 'Dog control'.

"You, my in-laws," he began. "I have come here to inform you that our marriage will not be consummated if we don't take good care of our dogs."

"From today onward," he continued. "I will control and monitor my dogs so that they don't come here. You should also do the same thing so that our marriage remains stable, otherwise, failing to control the dogs will lead us into communal disputes."

He concluded by saying dogs were idiots who liked looking at someone eating and liked eating food which was not given to them, and took things for granted. His in-laws were nodding their heads in approval of all he was saying because they knew at once that with his blood that high, the only option was to agree with him and avoid any further war of words. They replied to him positively despite the fact that the case was very uncertain. He was told respectfully to go home in peace and was assured that, they would monitor and take good care of their dogs so that he was not disturbed.

Thus, Kulang angrily left for his house. Luckily, one day, one of his in-laws' dogs came into his compound.

"Thank you Kuoth-Nhial (God of heaven)." he said to himself with a smile on his face. When he saw the dog, he took his weapon, threw it at the dog, and ran after it to the home of his in-laws. The dog was tired after running with Kulang, and it ran into the compound but he angrily threw a heavy stick at the dog in front of his mother in-law and the girl herself who was his wife-to-be. The dog ran into the *Luak*, but Kulang followed the dog inside the *Luak*.

He approached his father in-law.

"Didn't I tell you to monitor and control your dogs, my in-laws?" Kulang angrily asked. "Why didn't you respect our agreement by controlling your dogs when I have been respecting the agreement? Don't you know that our marriage will be destroyed by these dogs?" At that juncture, he left hurriedly.

A few days later, the family of the girl searched for reasons as to why Kulang got angry. They asked the girl if she had had some grievances with Kulang but found nothing. Finally, they discovered that Kulang needed the milk of his cow that he had paid as part of the dowry. The father ordered his daughters to milk the cows, put the milk in six gourds, and prepare food to be taken and given to the husband of their daughter, Kulang. The girls did as they were told by their father. They made everything ready including the milk of Kulang's cow which had given birth at their house.

At dawn, the girls left their home for Kulang's home and reached the village in the evening after walking a long distance. When they were about to reach the home, Kulang saw them from

When he saw the dog he took his weapon, threw it at the dog and ran after it to the last destination which was the home of his in-laws.

far and recognized his fiancée among them carrying things which made him smile because he knew his in-laws were carrying sweet things. Kulang went speedily to greet them because they were carrying edible goods. He was unable to close his teeth because of the happiness that filled his heart. He knew that his trick was discovered by his in-laws that he termed as, 'good in-laws.' His in-laws knew very well that Kulang always appreciated someone who refused food in his home or who gave him food.

After he welcomed the girls, he ordered Nyachom to cook for them a good meal. He slaughtered a fat he-goat for them to eat.

The food was mixed with Lieth-Yang (margarine) and the goat's meat was prepared by Nyachom and given to the girls who ate and became fully satisfied. In the following morning, the girls decided to leave. Kulang and other men escorted them to their home. Six days later, Kulang prepared some more food to compensate his in-laws for the food that they had sent to him. He filled eight gourds and a very big fish which were taken by his daughters to the family of his wife-to-be.

The girls finally reached their destination in the evening. They were warmly welcomed, served with water and food after which they went to sleep. In the morning, Kulang's father-in-law came to the girls and greeted them. He asked after the well-being of the family there including Kulang. He brought a cow and slaughtered it for the girls. The girls spent three days enjoying their stay, and finally went back and reported all the developments to Kulang who later gave maximum respect to his in-laws for the job well-done.

THREE

Kulang's Brother-in-Law is Killed

One day, during the hot summer season, Kulang's two brothers-in-law came to visit their sister Nyachom and her husband Kulang at their home village. They brought with them a heifer and put it together with Kulang's cattle.

Kulang wasn't at home by then when his in-laws came. He was busy tilling in his garden. Nyachom decided to make food for her two brothers who came to visit them. Since Kulang didn't authorize her to make food for her brothers, she hurried to make it before he could come home. Even though he couldn't cook as per Nuer custom, he regularly monitored and controlled the cooking procedures.

As the food reached to Nyachom's two brothers, Kulang appeared in the compound and surprised everyone and started to glare at the food as if his brothers-in-law didn't exist. Kulang did not greet them but instead popped out his eyes with anger wondering how Nyachom broke into the kitchen without his permission. He thought for a while and asked his two brothers-in-law a question sarcastically: "Is this Lieth of your heifer which your sister has given you just today?"

Kulang's question astonished the two brothers. They didn't answer it because they felt very disappointed to answer such question.

They wondered why someone who married their sister would treat them like strangers. After a while, he took his Thom, a traditional guitar, which he used to talk to his wife Nyachom, whenever he wanted to pass an urgent or confidential message regarding food, or if he wanted to insult whoever came home during meal time. Kulang started singing with the guitar:

"*e ding–ding-mi-te-di-ke-chieng-nyaal,mi keni dap goa, mi-chi-dap-thaar ka chi keede liw. Ka-han baa-pur-chi naath le nyak-ke-ngac-ka-han-baa kaka-chi-naath-le-nyak-ke-nen,ka-han-baa-konga-chi-naath-le nyak-ke-ngiec.*"

One of the things every man learned from Kulang was the language of his Thom. Ding! Ding! boomed the Kulang's Thom at intermissions.

Nyachom had lost her first born child the year before so Kulang was mocking his in-laws with why they were suddenly coming to eat in the house of a woman who had lost a child. Perhaps, he wanted them to cry and return instead of eating. How happy would Kulang be if the young men had only come to cry and return quickly?

After hearing all the insults in parables through guitar, the younger brother in-law became sad and left immediately and returned to their home village. The elder brother Bilbor remained with the husband of his sister. Later in the evening, Nyachom gave Kulang and Bilbor food together. Kulang sadly and angrily ate the food with his in-law, Bilbor, because he hated his brother-in-law's visit to the extent of sharing food with him and eating twice at his

When the war erupted between the two communities, Bilbor was killed on the spot,

home. When they finished eating, he went to sleep without saying good night to his brother in law. His face was as heavy as the face of someone in a funeral rite.

At dawn the next day, there was a report about a war that had erupted in the neighbourhood called Kuer-Buach, on the other side of the Chieng-Jaak Stream. The war was between Chieng-Geng, where Kulang belonged fighting against the Chieng-Jaak. Bilbor the brother in-law had to run with the young men of Chieng-Geng, to the battlefield because in the Nuer custom of war, one isn't allowed to remain at home or far away during war. Taking a side during a war is a must in the Nuer formal procedure of war. When the war erupted between the two communities, Bilbor was killed on the spot. Meanwhile, The Chieng-Geng community was defeated by Chieng-Jaak.

Sectional fight killing is not as complicated as murder in Nuer customary law. If a killing occurs in a declared sectional fight, it has a nature of defense. The compensation for the death as a result of a communal fight is usually fifty head of cattle as a fine and three years' imprisonment unlike the murder or intentional killing of a person who was not ready to fight. The compensation for the deceased is usually sixty head of cattle, imposing a fine of twenty head of cattle on the offender and ten years imprisonment of the offender. With that, Bilbor's killer had to pay fewer cattle because his death was purely accidental because he went to fight of his free will.

Upon returning home, the young men in sorrow disclosed the bad news of Bilbor's death to Kulang, who instead became happy because the previous night, his brother in-law was eating from his rations. When Nyachom heard of her brother's death, she deeply mourned and cried for the passing on of her brother.

"Did I hear someone crying or my ears are deceiving me?" Kulang asked himself. "Oh it is Nyachom's voice. Kuoth-Nhial, will people really eat tonight with that ceaseless cry?"

Kulang came and rebuked Nyachom when he heard her ceaselessly crying. The neighbours who came to comfort the family thought that Kulang was going to comfort his wife on her brother's death but they were wrong.

"Nyachom, Nyachom Loang!" said Kulang furiously. "Don't destroy my homestead with your cry, for I discovered your brother's death and cried last night when you gave us food together. I had a premonition and had known that Bilbor would die because he was randomly spooning from all the dish's corners taking huge swallows. People who don't know eating habits easily die, so don't destroy my home with the death of someone who didn't have manners while dining or follow him now."

Kulang strongly cautioned Nyachom who immediately ceased crying for her safety. After warning his wife he turned to the comforters: "Where is the person who broke the news before people eat?" he paused and waited for an answer while angrily looking at the crowd of mourners but no one spoke.

"It is not a good habit" he continued. "Disclosing bad news while people's stomachs are empty. Let that person change that habit or he will lose his life in the forthcoming death."

FOUR

The Fight over Hippo's Legs

Though most of the Nuer are pastoralist (centering their lifestyle on cattle rearing) they also carryout agricultural activities and fishing, to supplement their diet occasionally. They use local fishing methods using local technology to catch fish and to carryout farming.

The villagers, one particular day, were told that there was a fishing party where people could go fishing in the fishing places of Nyagool and Poon which were believed to have more fish. The people decided to go fishing en masse.

When they arrived, they placed their fishing nets in one of the tributaries where there was an abundant group of fish. In checking their nets in the morning hours, a little hippo was found trapped by the net. The net that had trapped the hippo was called Pathoot. Those who found the little hippo ran to the village to inform everybody about what had transpired. Unbeknownst to them, the little hippo had already died and the people decided to divide its meat among them.

When it was slaughtered, one of the young men said he needed the hippo's four legs so that he could give them to his uncle, Golongpin. The young man, after he was given the legs by the slaughterers, left for his uncle's home and handed the hippo's legs to him upon arriving.

"Thank you very much, nephew," the old man said. "But I cannot eat them alone without giving my friend, Kulang Toat. Now take two legs and give them to him. I shall remain with the other two legs."

When the young man handed the two hippo's legs to Kulang, he left. Kulang called his wife Nyachom and gave her some instructions regarding how to cook the two hippo's legs.

"Nyachom, Nyachom Loang!" Kulang called out. "I need you to cook my two hippo's legs, I know you like giving soup away to people but take care; I am warning you for the last time. I need my food untouched, my sister."

Nyachom then started as she was warned by her husband, Kulang. She put the two legs in the pot in the early morning and prepared a traditional food called 'Kop'. When she finished cooking 'Kop', she went to milk the cows.

While Nyachom was away milking cows, their dog Ken-Thiäng-dak went and sat around the pot, attracted by the smell of the legs of the hippo in the boiling pot. Unfortunately, the dog broke the pot and ate the two legs.

When Nyachom returned back she saw the dog slumbering around the pot. She knew that something was wrong. As soon as she found out that the dog had actually eaten everything, she cried in silence because she knew Kulang very well when it came to food.

Nyachom thought for a while and planned a trick to make Kulang a little bit happy.

"Yes," Nyachom said to herself. "I must prepare food for him so that I will be disclosing the news while he is busy eating."

She made delicious grilled meat to give to him as she couldn't disclose the bad news while Kulang wasn't eating something.

Nyachom at that moment sat down and gave him the food and said, "Please kill me, Father of my kids."

Upon hearing that, Kulang said "Okay! Let me eat my food after that I shall kill you." After he had eaten and became satisfied while expecting his two hippo's legs again not knowing that they were not there, Kulang said, "Nyaloang! Nyaloang! Why would I kill you my beautiful and caring wife? Even if you killed all my cows, burned down my *Luak* and the houses I wouldn't kill you, Just tell me the reason why you said I should kill you, don't fear, feel free, my darling." Kulang begged with a smile on his face.

Nyachom finally decided to unveil the bad news with eyes closed: "Your dog Ken-Thiäng-dak…," Nyachom paused as her voice was shaking with fear like someone disclosing the death of an important person.

"Talk, talk, please, my wife!" Kulang insisted on with sad heart as could be noticed by the frowns in his face.

"Well, it has eaten your two hippo's legs while I was away milking cows." Nyachom finally disclosed it while still trembling with fright.

Then and there in surprise and shock, Kulang jumped to his feet, blubbered and lamented: "*Dhor-Nyimaar-mi-ci-loch-tol-e-hok-kama-wini! wo! Nyachom! Nyachom Loang!* This is the only case that I kill women for. Your day is today, God has said you will not eat the grain and food of the next day." continued Kulang in rage. "Nyachom, Nyachom Loang! Die in peace! Let your soul rest in peace in the name of the God of my ancestors!" Kulang angrily concluded.

As he was collecting his spears, Nyachom ran and climbed a very big tree but Kulang took his axe, ran after her and started to cut down the tree.

Three men came to advise him not to kill his wife..

One of the men was Ruai Pab, his friend, who begged him not to kill his wife.

"Forgive her please." said Ruai.

"My friend Ruai Pab! Do you have something to give me today in your house or yours is just an empty advice?" Kulang angrily asked.

The second man cleared his throat and said, "Father of Chamkuan, please don't kill your wife."'

"You people of Thiäng," Kulang irately replied. "Why do you like to give empty advice to people? Take care and don't attempt to talk again. Just go home because you actually are vulnerable and unfit to advise real men with your bare hands. I will never listen to your fake advice since Nyachom let my hippo's legs be eaten by the dog. She will not live anymore. Today is her last day to see the sun."

A few minutes after the two men left while Kulang was busy cutting down the tree, the same man, Golongpin, who had sent him the two hippo's legs earlier, arrived with a very fat goat and the remains of the other two hippo's legs.

Nyachom ran and climbed a very big tree but Kulang took his axe, ran after her and started to cut down the tree that Nyachom had climbed on.

He began to call at Kulang with his clan name that every Nuer person likes.

"Can you leave what you are doing and take this goat home for your dinner?" Golongpin asked.

Golongpin didn't ask at all what had happened because he knew Kulang liked actions more than words. When Kulang returned after he took home the goat, Golongpin again gave him two hippo's legs and told him that the two legs were parts of the legs which were brought to him by his nephew.

When Kulang received the legs of the hippo, Golongpin asked him where Nyachom was. Kulang told him that Nyachom was in the tree. Then Golongpin told him to let her come down to take the legs home by herself.

When Nyachom came down from the tree, Kulang said to her, "Nyachom! My wife! I have nearly killed you for no reason while you were right, the dog was right, the legs were right, the pot was right and me, I was right."

Kulang visibly looked sad but he had to forgive the wife because of the food he had just received. Then he warned all those who gave empty advice with their bare hands that he would never listen to them for the rest of his life. He said he would only listen to Golongpin's advice or someone else who acted like him.

FIVE

Kulang's Sarcasm

In this world the behaviours of a selfish individual aren't easy to notice since they often appear really good, lovable and sweet. Really though, a selfish person only tries to satisfy their own pleasures as they have little consideration for other people's needs since they worry only about their own comfort. Most selfish people are skilled manipulators by nature who believe that they are more important than everyone else. They can hurt you very easily and you might feel confused and lost when you're around them as they make you feel like you aren't giving enough back to them.

Kulang slaughtered one of his cows in his home and his homestead was full of the vultures, kites and other birds which like the place of meat. The kite has a strong sight and it swoops down with its legs lowered to snatch small prey like chicks, rodents and fish before speedily return to the sky. Despite all this, the Nuer people believe that, the kite is one of the poorest birds in the world.

A superstition about kite says that the kite one day questioned the vulture on his usual attempt of withdrawal when he is stoned.

"My friend vulture," the kite called. "I have been observing you for so long. Why do you always withdraw whenever you are stoned by humans?"

"For my safety" he simply said. "But I am afraid you will one day be stoned with meat and you will miss it by running away."

The kite advised him that he should not withdraw when stoned even if he was stoned with a log fire or meat mixed with poison by children; he would catch it first because he is a bird that believes he can.

Kulang's visitor, Jok Ruai Yut, after he saw the slaughtered cow and the handful of birds, came and asked Kulang, who was busy separating the slaughtered cow's inner tissues from the outer ones. "Good morning." Jok greeted.

"It is not always good to say good morning when actually it's almost noon. Don't you know that it will be afternoon very soon?" Kulang replied sharply without looking at the man.

"Why have these more vultures and kites come in big number today?" said Jok.

"I thought you came with them and I was going to ask you this question if you did not hurry," Kulang simply replied. "If you have any vulture or kite that you recognize to be yours, take it, I have no time for silly questions."

Jock Ruai Yut ignored Kulang's silly answer and instead asked another question. "No, I did not come with them." Jok said with a forced smile. "May I taste the meat of your cow, brother Kulang?"

"... but you have just said that you didn't come with them and now you also need to taste the meat like these vultures." Kulang wondered. "I am very sorry to tell you that my elder son Chamkuan had tasted it yesterday so he said it was very sweet."

"How? Did he taste the meat yesterday before the cow was slaughtered?" asked Jok surprised.

"I have clearly said that you must be another clever vulture in the scene that has come to deceive me in the form of my friend Jok Ruai Yut." Kulang angrily said as he was ready to chase the man together with the vultures since he had now found an accusation calling him a 'vulture in the form of a human'.

To avoid the war of words, Jok remained silent and only asked the way to lead him to his village. "May you direct me to my destination?" Jok asked.

Finally, Kulang furiously replied and shouted his name, "Jok, Jok Ruai Yut! Are the roads made in my home? When did I become a company of the roads? Why don't you choose whichever can lead you out of my home? Our relationship is over if this is the way you ask questions. From today onward act as if you have never seen and known me before in life and with no doubt on my side as we are talking now, I have never seen and known your face or ever heard of your name. Who are you, Jok?"

Finally, Jok Ruai left in disappointment and Kulang became happy for letting the man go away without taking any meat.

Three months later, there was an old man who was believed to be a beggar in the land. He heard that Kulang never helped people, even though he was rich but he thought he would be given food by

*If you have any vulture or kite that you recognize to be yours, take it,
I have no time for silly questions.*

Kulang because he was poor. One day when Kulang slaughtered his goat, the old beggar arrived at his home.

"Please! Please! Give me some meat?" asked the beggar.

"No, I won't give you because meat comes from cow and cow comes from millet and millet comes after a hard work! Just follow your road, Gatgualen." Kulang replied roughly.

"I am a poor man, sir." the beggar replied sadly.

" Is 'Poor' a clan?" Kulang asked sarcastically.

"No, sir, poor is a person who has no resources." the beggar inoffensively replied.

"What do you mean?" Kulang asked surprised. "Were you born poor? I have never heard of someone who was born poor in my life."

"My parents passed away when I was young." replied the beggar with tears in his eyes as he reminded himself of his dead parents but Kulang instead asked him what he had been doing all that time since his parents had died when he was young and now he had grown up but the beggar could not understand Kulang's question in parable.

"Could you give me some milk or beans because I have been hungry for two days?" the beggar kept asking, forced by hunger against his dignity.

"I will never give you anything because you have eyes, legs and hands to help yourself but you chose to beg." Kulang said sharply.

"Okay I see," said the beggar. "But please give me some drinking water and I will go ahead."

"I don't have free water, Gar-guur." Kulang whispered. "Who doesn't know that water is found in the river in this world? It is only a mother who gives free water to her kids. But I am very sorry to tell you that I am not your mother."

"Oh, my dear cousin," cried the beggar. "Why are you sitting here then? Stand up and start begging meat, milk and water from the rich people. You are now even poorer than I am!" the beggar said after Kulang denied him everything including water which was always given for free across the land.

SIX

Kulang Burns the Walking Stick

It was in the middle of the rainy season, early morning when the clouds began to gather in the sky at the Toch village. Kids went out playing when it drizzled.

"*Chi Nhiaal deem kore-way-way! Nhial e demna, kore-wayway!*" the song of the kids repeated several times in their play as they enjoyed the little rain. As it was drizzling, a disabled man whose leg was amputated, arrived and leant on his wooden crutch as he could not go ahead to his destination for fear of the rain that was about to pour down heavily.

Finally, the rain changed from drizzling to torrential rain meanwhile the kids, after experiencing the different between the drizzling and the torrential rain, ran to their mothers' huts. Kulang on the other hand went to his *Luak* without inviting the disabled man in who had decided to stop temporarily in the village.

Nhial Puot who was the disabled person decided to follow Kulang inside his *Luak* as it was raining heavily outside, even though he was not invited by Kulang. Since it was raining heavily, the firewood for cooking was soaked in water. When Kulang saw his uninvited guest, he went to the garden and brought some maize for two of them.

After he came back from the farm, he found out that the disabled man had fallen asleep. Kulang secretly took the wooden crutch that supported the disabled man, broke it, and made fire out of it in order to roast the maize that he had brought from his farm. After roasting the maize, Kulang woke up his visitor cheerfully: "*Nhial! Nhial!* Get up and eat some maize, Gatgualen." he called out.

They ate the well roasted maize and became satisfied. When they finished all the maize, Kulang began the conversation by praising the disabled man who didn't know that his crutch was burnt.

"Nhial! You are one of the best visitors." Kulang said. "Please come home whenever you want."

The disabled man became happy and decided to leave. He told Kulang that he had to go home and sleep in Rup-Nhial on the other side of the river. He thanked Kulang for the accommodation and the nice words. When he finished, he stretched his hand out to where he had put his crutch before but it wasn't there.

Then he respectfully turned to Kulang: "Uncle Gat-Toat, did some kids come here when I was sleeping?" asked the disabled man.

"Why have you asked such question?" Kulang instead asked him back.

The disabled man said his wooden crutch was missing, for he wanted to know if the kids took it out or not.

Kulang put a smile on his face and said, "Nhial! Nhial Puot! The maize that you were eating, wasn't it well roasted? How come you didn't refuse the maize? You could not like both maize and Crutch. You should have liked one at the expense of the other."

The disabled man politely replied and said, "I have accepted what you have done to me and as I have nowhere to go since I am a disabled person, I will have to spend the rest of the autumn season in your house and we shall be eating together."

Kulang's eyes popped out when he heard the speech of the disabled man about eating with him continuously. "Let's see if there will be no fight?" Kulang warned.

The disabled man had to stay with Kulang but when they spent some days eating together in the same dish, Kulang became confused of what to do since the man had lost his walking crutch. Kulang became puzzled and miserable because the man used to eat a lot of food. After some thought, Kulang decided to go to a small town called Toch in Thiäng area of Fangak, in order to buy another wooden crutch from the Arab traders. Kulang sold one of the best goats he had in order to buy the crutch. When he returned home, he gave the disabled man the new crutch that he had bought from Toch town, because he wanted to bring to an end his miseries of sharing food with his uninvited guest. Kulang knew very well that, the consequences of an act affect the likelihood of it happening again.

When the disabled man received his walking crutch, he told Kulang that he would have stayed with him for a long time if he hadn't bought his crutch.

"*Ngoth Ka Baaw!*" he joked when he saw frowns on Kulang's face like a chicken soldier expecting a heavy battle against the enemy. "You know very well as I do, that I am a disabled person and yet you used my crutch for cooking maize. I am very sad indeed that

Kulang secretly took the wooden crutch that supported the disabled man, broke it and made fire out of it in order to roast the maize.

your own making victimized you because I spent some days eating with you and finally you sold out the fattest billy goat that you had in order to buy a wooden crutch for me."

The disabled man told him a story that happened before and said: 'There was once a man who played a trick just like you did. It rained heavily for the whole day and no firewood was available for cooking as all the firewood was soaked in water. All the cows weren't milked because the calves and the young ones were with their mothers.

"When the wives of that man called Chuaal Pech came to him in order for them to be given one Thir-*Luak* (a tall and thick tree's branch that supports the *Luak* from inside) for the food to be cooked, he refused, consequently, the whole family including the man slept without food. Then Chuaal Pech said his trick had made him suffer as a result since he never gave it a thought that the trick would be the opposite of what he was expecting."

In the end, the disabled man waved goodbye to Kulang, who was just looking helplessly at him without talking because he feared the man would again wait for the evening meal which would possibly make Kulang go crazy. The disabled man told him to remain in peace with his wife and his son Chamkuan.

SEVEN

Kulang Dismisses his Friend

Sharing of food among the Nuer is very common and it is considered part of the tradition. A meal is shared in the same village and beyond especially among the members of neighbouring homesteads and hamlets.

Kulang and one of his best friends, Ruai Pab, were two good friends who used to walk and eat together in their village. The two friends were so different that, people in the village wondered if they had any mutual topics to talk about because everyone knew Kulang very well. Whenever the food was brought by their wives, Kulang would give his dog a big chunk of food approximately four times because he wanted to annoy and disown Ruai Pab as a friend, for he was fed up of sharing his ratio of food and eating with him. But Ruai Pab did not usually give him any chance to because he was a kind human who knew how to put up with the habits of people like Kulang.

As Africans say, "When a hyena wants to eat its children, it first accuses them of smelling like goats." Kulang really wanted a reason to accuse his friend because no matter how strong somebody is, he cannot approach and disown someone without a reason. A mere reason to convince oneself outwardly in front of people but inwardly and alone, one would even be a witness of himself that it didn't hold any ground.

After he failed in all his tricks to annoy and chase his friend, one night, the two friends were chatting as they usually did while waiting for their dinner from their wives. The night was very bright because there was moonlight and mosquitoes were disturbing the ears of the two good friends. Kulang reminded his friend of the kids' superstition story about the Ear and the Mosquito.

"Kids are stupid like their mothers." Kulang said.

"How is that, cousin?"

"Are you kids or kids' mothers, Ruai?"

"None of them"

"Then why do you defend them?"

"I have not. But I want to know the reason that qualifies them to be stupid."

"Then, why are you always quick?"

"Okay sorry."

"What is the benefit of 'Sorry'?" Ruai kept silent to avoid the further war of words.

Now after Kulang had satisfied himself that Ruai did not want the debate to move on and he knew he would not get rid of Ruai in that situation, he narrated the whole story on why the kids were stupid like their mothers. He hoped to get a reason to get rid of his friend especially by questioning the reality of the story but he was wrong as Ruai would not do so.

"They always tell a story about the nature of the Mosquito and the Ear which goes like this:" he began.

"The Ear was the most radiant beauty in the whole world. It was normal that everyone wanted to marry her and the Ear had become used to prospective grooms challenging them to a fight. She was just too beautiful; the poor, weak, as well as small creatures knew to stay away, all except the Mosquito. The Mosquito had a crazy crush on the Ear. Finally, he told his feelings to the Ear but the Ear felt insulted and said, 'Mosquito how dare you, who is considered to be the weakest of all creatures. How dare you even think about marrying me? Can't you see these entire brave and wealthy young men who have come to lay their lives for me? Do you honestly think I will pick you over anyone of them? You, whom I am sure, will be dead within a week!'

"The Ear's speech made all the suitors to laugh leaving the poor Mosquito ashamed and humiliated. 'Dead in a week?' said Mosquito. 'We shall see about that'. The weeks went by and mosquito didn't die; years went by and he was still alive. Now whenever Mosquito sees the Ear, he approaches her and buzzes, 'I am still alive, Nyame'."

"It is a good story, cousin." Ruai overrated and compromised so as not to anger him, leaving Kulang sad after he told a long story but didn't get a reason to chase his friend away who had instead appreciated the good story.

"…but it is not my story." he said, trying to create a pandemonium by challenging his friend's appreciation on a story which was not his but he knew it would be stupid to do so. He thought of another trick to make him end the relationship since it was the last day for him after he failed several times.

SKulang Dismisses his Friend

My friend Ruai! Look at the moon, it has come out today.

Although the mosquitos were disturbing them, Kulang started another topic about the moon which had come out four days before and said, "My friend Ruai! Look at the moon - it has come out today"

Ruai with no clue of Kulang's trick, replied. "But this moon has been there for four days now, brother."

With Ruai's response, Kulang became happy in finding a reason to let him go because he knew he would easily twist Ruai's answer to look rude. At that point, he faked an irritation and cleared his throat loudly pugnaciously.

"Oh! Oho! Ay! Ruai! Ruai Pab! Why do you always oppose whatever I say?" he said while shaking with the recently faked anger. "How do you say the moon has been out for four days when it came out only today? Is that not a lie from you, Ruai Pab? If this is the way you behave then each of us must have his moon in his home because we cannot share one home whose moon arises differently. From now on, I want you to take your cows and anything that belongs to you and go. Pack and go please, Ruai! Now! Now! Not later. I am tired of your infinitive arguments always while you are younger than me. I cannot entertain your negative lifestyle full of arguments and oppositions. These are my words. Only dogs are allowed to visit each other in this Chieng-Geng land. It is over between us forever even if the Sky and the Earth collide, we will never be friends again." Kulang angrily concluded, and he was shaking in an anger that he had just counterfeited up.

From there, their friendship came to an end and Kulang was

happy as he continued eating alone to his satisfaction without anyone on the other side of the dish. Kulang did not know that he who tosses away a friend is as bad as he who tosses away his life.

EIGHT

Kulang Expels his Son

One day, Kulang called his son Chamkuan for a meeting. "My son," he said. "Why do you always come home alone? Don't you have any friend in this Thiäng-land?"

Chamkuan was going to talk in defense of himself when Kulang continued his offensive speech.

"If I were you, I wouldn't come home without friends. When I was at your age, I used to walk with more friends and I was already fending for myself. Your name alone defines who you are because Chamkuan means someone whose life depends on eating food alone. I have done my best to make you grow into kulang, but there is too much of Nyachom in you. You have no room in my heart, son of woman." Kulang challenged his son with a loud voice so that he would have friends.

So, the son listened to all that his father had said. When they finished talking, his son left his father's place.

The real fact as to why Chamkuan didn't use to come home with friends was because of Kulang's egotistical behaviours in Thiäng-land. Chamkuan thought that Kulang would have become angry with him if he had brought friends home for he was a good boy who respected all. Kulang was believed to be the number one in self-centeredness in and around Thiäng-land.

Kulang Expels his Son

The following day, Chamkuan went to his friends, after they finished their conversation, he told four of his friends that they should go to his father's homestead together. The four accepted the request of Chamkuan. When the young men approached the home, Kulang saw his son Chamkuan with other four boys. He then called his wife Nyachom. He told Nyachom to cook a very good meal urgently for her son and his peers. Nyachom prepared and served Chamkuan and his friends with a very nice, mixed and delicious meal of two dishes as ordered by her husband Kulang. After they ate, they became happy and content. They spent the whole day chatting happily together. In the evening, the four youth decided to leave so they talked to Kulang for them to leave officially. Kulang told them that, his home was theirs and any time they would be welcome home.

"Go in peace my sons and thank you for coming to us." Kulang said cheerfully.

Chamkuan escorted his peers and returned. The following morning, Kulang called Chamkuan for the evaluation of his peers' visit.

"Chamkuan! Son of my wife," Kulang irritably called out. A change from Chamkuan Kulang to Chamkuan Nyachom as most men do when kids' social or academic performance becomes poor.

"Why did you put me in shame? Why did you bring only four people to my house when you know very well that I know the garden work very well? The reason why I work hard is for you." Kulang angrily continued challenging his son. "I have a lot of cows and everything, for that reason, you cannot come with only four people but because you know that you are the worst son of a woman and that is why you have no enough friends in this Thiäng-land." he furiously told his son who said nothing out of respect.

The following day, after Kulang had finished instructing his son, Chamkuan came home with six more friends. Kulang ordered Nyachom to cook good food for them. The youth became happy for being fully accommodated by the family of Chamkuan with open hands.

When the youth left, Kulang called his son Chamkuan for the second time and said, "Son of Nyachom! Chamkuan! Why have you again put me in shame by coming with few people, my son? You are a selfish who has no friend; you have no girlfriend and will never marry in this Thiäng-land. You are someone whose power is from hand to mouth. You were initiated to adulthood longtime ago and still behave like someone who is not. Chamkuan you don't know even fishing in the river and don't know work because you are being misled by your mother who is my wife by giving you delicious food every day. You actually are expert in courting girls at night in the village. You must leave my house, because you are a disobedient boy."

When Kulang finished insulting him, he cried throughout the night. Nyachom also became sad because her grown-up son was put to shame with insults. The following morning, the Englishmen came to their village and took all the able men to do the dykes and tarmac roads work in the place called Wiech-dier. Chamkuan was taken but his father wasn't taken because he was an old man.

After working for a long time, the Englishmen decided that the workmen should have a break. Chamkuan invited twelve youth to go and rest at their home. The twelve youth accepted Chamkuan's request and they left together toward Kulang's home. The moment the young people were about to reach the home, Kulang was busy collecting cow manure. He finally recognized his son walking with twelve other young men - thirteen in all. Kulang was soon seen put down his tilling tools and started to glare at the people coming home from afar.

As soon as he noticed and satisfied himself that the twelve young men were coming home with Chamkuan, he called his son in a loud voice and said, "Why don't you guys sing a war song because we are at war now? Where is your war lead singer? Chamkuan, you have come to attack my home with these warriors!"

He then ran to his Luak, brought his weapons, jumped like someone in the battlefield, cried 'Walilili' and alerted Nyachom that they were under attack and that she must get prepared for the fight against the invaders. The young men became surprised as they stood in one place in fear, for if they tried to move forward or backward, Kulang would throw spears at them.

Kulang started to talk angrily to Chamkuan and his peers when he satisfied himself that the youth stood still. "Chamkuan! Chamkuan Nyachom," said Kulang with heavy voice. "Why did you bring the whole world to my house? Go away with your hundreds of friends, for my life isn't dedicated to feeding the Chieng-Geng community in this Thiäng-land. If you have any portion in my garden, please take it with your friends from around the world. There is no food for you and your friends. If you feel like to feed them go and level your own garden, Chamkuan."

He then turned to the boys: "What about you, hundred mouths?" he said, describing them as 'mouths' instead of people. "Lazy guys of Chamkuan, what does your friend give me? Your friend Chamkuan has no garden; he doesn't know how to till land. Last year, his garden near the forest was controlled by weeds in his presence; he is now eating our food with my lovely wife, Nyachom. His life is dependent on me in this world. He doesn't know how to make food for himself so he stays near me so that he benefits and survives through me because he is lazy. He cannot even carry a bundle of maize. Now you go to your respective homes. These are my words about your friend Chamkuan who knows only the eating and drinking milk of my cows and goats."

Afterwards, Chamkuan and the boys became ashamed and depressed for they were badly insulted. The youth left to their homes very disappointed. Chamkuan became hopeless because he had brought friends at first when his father insulted him for coming with few but when he had brought twelve more men his father had insulted him in their presence and called them enemies, the whole Chieng-Geng community and the entire world.

From that time onwards, Chamkuan never came home with anyone until when his father Kulang died in1968 in Longtem. Chamkuan was also believed to have inherited some of his father's behaviours as the Nuer elders said: 'A cow resembles its young one.'

Kulang Expels his Son

Chamkuan, you have come to attack my home with these warriors!

NINE

Kulang Apprehends Sugar

There is a saying: 'You can take a villager out of the village but you cannot take a village out of him.'

One day, one of Kulang Toat's nephews by the name Pel, came to his home while Kulang was still tilling in the garden. Pel saw Kulang's water-pot and put some sugar into it without the knowledge of Nyachom. When Kulang returned home, he requested some drinking water because he was thirsty. When he was given the water, he tried to rinse his mouth first before he could drink. He then realized that the water was very sweet and nice and he swallowed it and smiled. Kulang drank all the water.

He then called Nyachom again with a smile on his face "Queen Nyaloang," he happily said. "Mother of my son Chamkuan! Which place in the river did you get this water from?" Nyachom told him that it was the same place in the river that she used to fetch water from since Nyachom had no knowledge about the sugar that was put in the water. Kulang asked her to bring all the water in the pot so that he could drink it.

"You have never in your life fetched as sweet as this water, mother of my kids." Kulang told Nyachom thankfully.

When he drank all the water; he sent Nyachom to go to the same tributary and fetch the same water in the same place. Nyachom left and brought water but when he tried to drink the water, he found that the taste was not as sweet as the first pot of water. So he yelled in disbelief.

"*Wo! Woo!* Nyachom! Nyachom Loang! How did you miss the point where you fetched the first water from, my beautiful wife?"

The '*Wo*' sound is the sound of hopelessness. When someone suddenly died, people would shake their heads for a long time, saying, '*Wo! Wo! Wo!*' just as Kulang had now said.

He then poured out the water. Kulang didn't know that the first pot of water was mixed with sugar by his nephew who came from town, and Nyachom, was not also informed about that.

Kulang sent his wife again to the river and warned her. "Nyachom!" Kulang called out. "Go and bring me sweet drinking water, if you don't you will leave my house. Go exactly where you fetched from at first. I will be waiting as I know you always disobey instructions but this case is different as it may end someone's life."

When Kulang's nephew, Pel, who put sugar into Kulang's water-pot knew that Nyachom was in trouble from Kulang because of the sweet water that she would not find, he called her and said "Excuse me grandmother Nyachom! Please come to me. Don't suffer in Kulang's hand for something you can't get. Come and I will give you sugar. I have brought it from town. It is a substance that is mixed with water."

Now Nyachom became happy because she had been in a life-threatening situation. Finally, Kulang's water-pot was given an amount of sugar and was taken to him inside his Luak. When he tasted the water he found that the water was so sweet like the first water. Subsequently, he loudly laughed and became happy. "Queen Nyachom, Mother of my kids, where did you get it from again please?" Kulang said to his wife.

Many villagers who were with him became surprised of what inspired Kulang to laugh loudly and became happy for the first time after a very long time.

"The substance that made the water to become sweet was brought by your nephew Pel Nya-Toat from town and it is called 'sugar'." Nyachom told him.

At that juncture, Kulang called his nephew and said, "Pel! Son of my lovely sister! What do you call the substance that turns the tasteless water sweet? Is it a miracle?"

His nephew Pel answered him and whispered, "Uncle, that substance is called sugar in town; it is mostly used in making something called tea. It is also put in food."

Kulang thought a lot after he knew about what turns water to something sweet. In the night he didn't sleep because of the new substance called 'sugar'. He wished it could be planted in gardens just like crops such as maize and millet so that he could produce more of it.

The following morning, Kulang went to his garden. When he returned home, he called his nephew and asked him again.

"Nephew," he called. "The real son of my sister! Which town did you bring that sweet substance from? Tell me please, my dear?"

"I brought it from Arab traders in Fangak town." Pel replied. "Okay thank you!" he said. "Now take my best black expecting cow for sale in Fangak town so that you can buy that sweet substance which changes the tasteless water to sweet." Pel took the cow and sold it for four Sudanese Pounds.

After Pel sold out the cow, he bought four sacks of sugar each for one Sudanese Pound. Pel left and spent one night in the river transporting four sacks of sugar to his uncle. The following day, he arrived with the four sacks of sugar. When Kulang received the four sacks of sugar he became extremely happy with his nephew.

The next day, Kulang planned an urgent meeting with all his neighbours. The people came to his house wondering what Kulang was up to. All the people sat down and he cleared his throat to begin his speech in the meeting.

"You people of this village," he began. "Listen to me very well, this is the first and the last message. From today onward, we must divide the water-point where we collect our drinking water from. Each and every one of us must make a fence to protect the water point in the river and everyone must fetch only from the place he fenced. Note that we won't fetch water randomly from now onward. These are my first and the last words, goodbye." Kulang concluded the meeting in a hurry.

As soon as their meeting ended, the villagers were surprised at the agenda that had been raised by Kulang, concerning the fencing of the river which was believed to be impossible due to its continuous flow. After the villagers left, Kulang again called a meeting with his family members with the same agenda of dividing and fencing the water point.

"Now, we are all the family members of Kulang Toat. My message is that we must divide and fence our water point. You,

Nyachom, and your kids must have your part in the river and my part as well. This is what we must do and goodbye." he said.

Upon hearing that, Nyachom wasn't surprised at all. She knew her husband very well. "What is the motive behind the division and fencing of the water point which has never happened anywhere in the village?" Nyachom asked him.

"Okay, woman," Kulang replied. "Let me tell you the reason, Nyachom Loang. The behaviour of you women in this world is like the behaviour of chickens. You have no discipline and you do not listen to what the head of your family says. That is the reason why our water point must be divided."

When he finished talking to Nyachom, he left his house for the bushes and he cut big trees with his axe for fencing and dividing the water point. Thereafter, he returned and surprised his family members by fencing and dividing the water point. When he finished his work in the river he had a break. After he had rested, he took the four sacks of sugar and poured them into the river that he had divided thinking that the water in the river would be as sweet as the water of the day before, so that he could drink from it all the time.

After he poured the four sacks of sugar into the river, he went home happily and slept smiling waiting for the morning so that he could drink the sweet water. Insomnia might have attacked him as he was happily looking forward to the morning.

In the early morning, he brought his cows out from inside the *Luak*. When he finished, he took his big cup and went to the river so that he could drink. He took some water to drink and as he put

After he had taken rest, he took the four sacks of sugar and poured them into the river.

the water in his mouth he found out that it wasn't sweet anymore. He shouted with a loud voice that was heard by all the neighbours and beyond:

"*Woo! Woo! Woo! Waa! Waa! Waa! Oy! Oy!Oy!*" he cried with desolation. "My black nice cow had gone in vain without getting something from it. Pel! Pel my nephew the sugar is dead."

When his nephew heard that he came and asked him what had happened.

"What have you done with the sugar?" Pel asked. "I have poured the sugar into the river at the water point that I had fenced, and the taste of water remains tasteless." answered Kulang with tears rolling down his face.

Pel put him down and said, "Uncle, sugar is never poured in the river. Sugar cannot be put in a big quantity of water. It is put in small cups of tea or jugs of milk. It would have been good if you had just put it in a small amount of water in a cup or jug, uncle. You have now misused your sugar. You should have asked me first before dumping all four sacks of sugar in the water."

———

Kulang had done like a man in the Nuer fables who unwisely misused what God had given him. His name was Wadhaw. A great famine hit the land and people were reduced to eating low-grade fruits including weeds' roots and water lilies. One night as Wadhaw was hungrily sleeping in his hut, a gazelle that was in search of water entered his *Luak*.

In the morning, Wadhaw realized that God had given him easy prey in his *Luak*. He thanked God for helping him.

"Since God sent it purposely to me, I must not scratch or give holes to its skin so that I can make a good sleeping mat out of it." he thought loudly, as he was preparing his spears in order to slaughter it.

He closed the door and started to go to the gazelle but it resisted. Wadhaw wanted to catch and slaughter the gazelle with his knife for the safety of its skin which he wanted for making a sleeping mat. The brawl went on for sometimes between Wadhaw who wanted to catch the gazelle alive and the gazelle that was resisting. The two became tired at last. Unfortunately, the gazelle got an open space and left speedily leaving poor Wadhaw disappointed.

"I will only guarantee what I have eaten in this world." Wadhaw desperately said. Wadhaw left behind a powerful message advising people not to dance or be hopeful for something until it is guaranteed.

Nyachom became extremely sad because the only favourite cow of her kids was sold out for something that was wasted. A person having little knowledge does much harm to himself as well as to others. It is true that many people hate to ask others for help. They think that they can do things on their own.

In life, when things become difficult at home women normally say call someone to help with a solution but men say they can do it themselves even though they don't know how to go about it. At work, some people have a load of work to do, but they don't ask their co-workers for assistance. If we don't ask, we will be unable to find our valuable things just like Kulang lost all his sacks of sugar.

TEN

Kulang and the Four Feasts

One day, Kulang, received four important invitations for feasts from different homes at the same time. The owners of the homes sent their respective kids with verbal invitation messages.

The first invitation was for a feast in which a big fish was being cooked in honour of Kulang as the chief guest. The second invitation was for a feast in which a traditional white wine was being prepared in honour of Kulang. The third invitation was for a feast in which a castrated he-goat was being slaughtered in honour of Kulang. The fourth invitation was for a feast in which a fat cow was being slaughtered in honour of Kulang.

These invitations were delivered by different kids as it's a common custom in the Nuer culture to send kids with spoken messages to the neighbours, friends and relatives. Kulang was to make these competitive choices for feasts taking place on the same day at the same time. The four kids were sent differently by their respective parents but they arrived at the same time in the morning. The kids relayed their messages to Kulang who received these invitations with a smile and gratitude.

"I have been sent by my dad to inform you that you should come because a big fish was cooked in your honour." said the first kid, who arrived early in the morning at Kulang's home.

The second kid said, "I have been sent by my dad to invite you for the white wine that was made for the God of the land and you are being invited as one of the lead elders to bless the occasion."

The third kid said, "My father said you should come because he had slaughtered a fat goat last night and you are being expected this morning."

The fourth kid whispered, "My dad said I should tell you that you should come home as soon as you can for a feast."

When the kids finished conveying their separate messages to Kulang, they left and he became extremely happy indeed for the wonderful messages he had received that morning. After the gesture, Kulang became totally confused as to which place he should visit first, since all the four feasts were being done at the same time with competing and attractive offers of food and drinks.

Kulang became sad and confused and wished he could attend all the feasts in person at pleasure time to enjoy the bumper harvest. Kulang devised a plan to attend all these separate and conflicting invitations at once.

"Oh! How much better it would be if I could divide myself into four persons and each could attend these feasts at pleasure time so that my mind and stomach would be at peace." Kulang thought to himself.

In the process of trying to attend to all four functions, Kulang, walked and arrived at an intersection point that divided the four roads—each leading to these separate four functions. He first put his left leg to the first road which led to the place of the biggest banquet involving fish and his right leg to the road which led to

In the process of trying to attend to all four functions, Kulang walked and arrived at an intersection point that divided the four roads.

the place of the white wine, while his hands where pointing to the other two directions which led to the other two places. Kulang put his legs between two roads because each journey's end led to a very important feast. He didn't want to miss each of them for if he left the other three feasts for one, he would be unable to find them. Then with a faint voice, he called Nyachom and said, "Mother of Chamkuan! What shall I do now with all these beautiful roads? I don't want to miss each of them."

When his wife Nyachom saw that Kulang was in such confusion over the four roads leading to the feasts, she said, "Relax my husband, I will now go to the three places and inform them that you would be coming. Now go to the place of the fat cow's feast in the house of Guek Juch, because as per our tradition, across Nuer land and beyond, the meat from the cow's udder is the old men's favourite meat and for that reason you won't be waiting long like in the other places."

Kulang smiled and said, "Yes! Yes! That is the real solution for the problem, mother of Chamkuan, and my life, thank you very much for your help. Run Nyachom! Run! Let's exactly do that."

When Kulang quickly reached the road which led to the feast of fat cow's udder, he found many old men. He was greeted and called with his clan name.

"Owner of the hornless grey bull," greeted one man.

"*Maale?*" "*Maale mi goa,*" Kulang greeted back uninterestingly "Guys did you sleep here?"

"No! We didn't but we came in the early morning." replied another old man.

"I didn't expect that there would be so many guests as these?" he said, in a low voice that was heard only by those who were close to him because he hated large gatherings.

Kulang asked them because he was suspecting them to have eaten the meat in his absence but his doubts were proved wrong. The woman fully served them with meat when she saw Kulang arrive.

Kulang then speedily ran to the feast of the castrated goat. Fortunately, some part was kept for him until he arrived. After that he had to run to the feast of the big fish and found that the owner of the house was waiting for him. The wife served them with fish and he became extremely satisfied. He thanked the owner of the house for his hospitality and said, "What you have done has never been done before. May you live long to do it always."

Thereafter, he asked the owner of the house that he wouldn't prolong the conversation with him as he was in a hurry. Kulang still wanted to go to the last and final feast involving the white wine. He waved 'goodbye' to the owner of the house and left in hurry.

As soon as he arrived to the last feast, he found all men had drunk two big pots and left a pot for him and the owner of the house. Luckily, the owner of the house kept the whole pot of wine for him. Therefore, Kulang enjoyed the wine alone and became very happy. In the evening Kulang thanked the owner of the house and decided to leave.

"This day! This day! This day," Kulang said. "You will never be forgotten and you deserve annual commemoration because an enjoyment day as such has never happened in my whole life. I have never enjoyed like today since I was born by Toat Kang and Nyadoak Kier. I have found the foods which were made at the same time."

ELEVEN

Kulang Succumbs to Treachery

Kulang had a Loth (an ox's bell) which was believed to be the best of all across the Nuer land by that time. Every balang wanted to borrow or take it from him in order to court as many beautiful girls as possible. Singers were more liked by girls than the handsome and well built-up men who did not have traditional songs.

Many with sweet tongues and good approach came and spent some days with Kulang in order to please him so that they were given the loth. Everyone would tirelessly till in Kulang's garden for the whole day before returning for meal at Kulang's home. But when they finally disclosed the object of their visit, Kulang would not give his loth to them for he was half happy and half sad. He was happy for being helped in tilling and sad for being helped in eating. Many energetic youth with sweet tongues tried different styles on winning the Kulang's loth but were to no avail. It was now declared by all the people that none would get the loth from Kulang other than perhaps the unborn generation because more than ten motivational speakers and the wisest men of different lands had failed to do so.

Finally, a man called Machar Tot came home to visit Kulang. When he reached the house of Kulang in the morning, he found him tilling and removing weeds in the garden. Machar joined him and worked with him in the garden until noon and they rested. Kulang became very happy with Machar for helping him.

"My son!" he called. "What is your name and where are you from?"

"My name is Machar Tot; I am from Lil-Chieng-Kuoth, the next village." The visitor replied.

Kulang called Nyachom and told her to cook a very nice meal for his good friend, the important guest. Nyachom prepared a nice and delicious food called '*Kop*' (a traditional food meant for very important guests) and gave it to the guest who was sitting with Kulang inside the *Luak*. To Kulang's surprise, Machar refused to eat.

Kulang happily asked him with smile in his face and said, "Is it true that you don't eat it, aha?" then he told Nyachom again to do another nice type of food as soon as possible. Another delicious dish was prepared by Nyachom and was given to Machar who again refused it.

"Sorry," said Machar, "I don't eat beans, Guadinda."

Then Kulang with smile in his face said, "Aha! Nyachom! What are we going to do to this good friend? Anyway, put them up there for me I will eat them later."

At that moment, Kulang told Nyachom to cook a very nice Nuer dish called '*Walwal*' (a traditional light-porridge food) for Machar. Finally, Machar ate the simple food and Kulang became happy with the guest who refused expensive foods and ate food that was simple.

When Machar Tot finished eating, he talked to Kulang, and said, "Guadinda! I have made this journey for you in your house. I only need the Loth of your Chot-nyanga bull."

"My son!" he called, "Do you only need the 'Loth' of my ox? Is it the purpose for coming here? Well, it is there in the roof of the *Luak*, take it now."

At that moment, Machar Tot brought down the Loth from the roof of the *Luak*. Kulang told him to try it. When Machar tried it, the sound was the best of all sounds in the land. Machar Tot jumped and crooned with his traditional song because of happiness.

Machar Tot was an excellent *balang* (singer or someone who knows how to convince ladies) like Bol Phal Muang whose name reached the Gajaak, Gajiok, Lak, Leek, Nyuong, Jagei, Dok, Gawär, Haak, Bul and Lou-Nuer lands. Kulang became happy for the song of his friend, Machar. Machar Tot wouldn't have taken the Loth if he had eaten the nice and delicious foods with Kulang. But because he came for a reason, he pretended that he didn't eat good foods.

Kulang Succumbs to Treachery

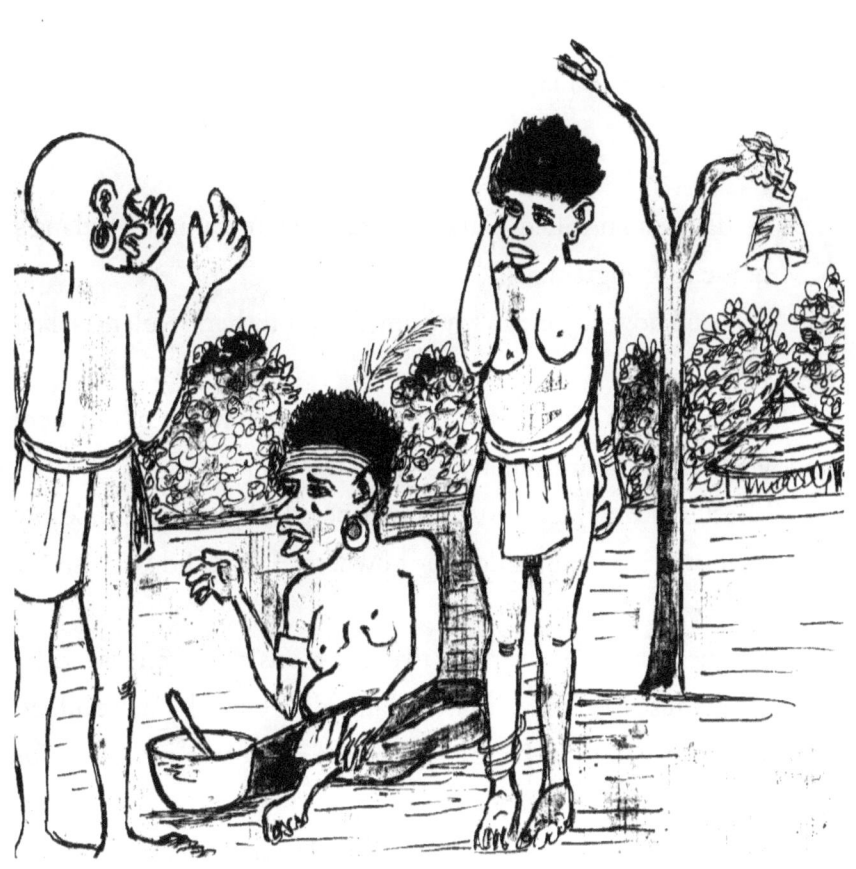

Sorry, I don't eat beans.

TWELVE

Kulang Suffers Revenge

One day, a man called Gatkuoth Ruei Wuor came to Kulang's home in Longtem.

"Do you know anyone in my home here, brother?" Kulang asked the visitor.

"I am only just a guest who ended up in the middle of nowhere and here I am in your home." answered the man.

"Middle of nowhere," Kulang whispered, "How did you know that my home is in the middle of nowhere? What did you use for discovering it?"

The guest didn't answer the two questions that were asked by Kulang because he knew that Kulang didn't need him. Kulang allowed him to sleep at his house but the night was mournful for the two, Kulang and Gatkuoth.

The following morning, Nyachom made a delicious food mixed with Lieth-yang (butter) for the two men, Kulang and the man who broke into his home the day before. While they were eating, Kulang twisted the dish to his side such that he could eat the side with milk and Gatkuoth could not eat it.

As they continued eating, Kulang asked Gatkuoth a very weird question. "My friend, Wikdinglieeth," he began "Do you have cows, grain and other types of wealth in your home?"

The visitor confidently replied and said, "Owner of Chot-nyanga bull! I am not here to tell you how rich or poor I am, I am just visiting your home."

In the evening, they were again given food by Nyachom. Kulang repeated more silly questions concerning food. When they finished eating, he went to sleep leaving his visitor Gatkuoth alone and sad. Kulang did not want to share food with him.

A story in Nuer is told that, there was a rich man called Mayian-Barchiang, who had a wife and many children. In one of the seasons, there was a drought and famine in the land that didn't allow people to grow crops for a while. Hunger hit the land of Mayian, but it was hard for a typical Nuer man to slaughter cattle for food. Cattle were meant for milk. A Nuer man would prefer to eat a cow that died accidentally then to slaughter a cow because of hunger.

The Nuer people, like other neighbouring Nilotic tribes, never eat cattle just because they want to. Cattle are very holy to the Nuer people, for that reason, when they do eat cattle they honour its spirit. Nuer people typically just eat the cattle that are old in age or dying because of sickness. But even if they do so, they all gather together performing rituals, dances or songs before and after they slaughter the cow. Never do they just kill cattle for the fun of it. Never does a Nuer person slaughter an animal exclusively for the desire to eat meat. There is the danger of the ox's spirit visiting a curse on any

While they were eating, Kulang twisted the dish to his side such that he could eat the side with milk.

individual who would slaughter it without formal procedure intent, aiming only to use it for food.

Mayian, heard that one of his neighbour's cattle was badly attacked by a lion in the bush and he went expecting to be given some meat. Unfortunately, as famine destroys hearts, including the good ones, the man refused to give Mayian, even a single piece of meat. After that Mayian became sad.

"Well, my friend, Life is long," he said. "The lion did not die and it may attack my cattle next time."

That excerpt means everyone eventually has to face up to the consequences of his actions. We all could face the same outcomes that we impose on others in a good or bad way.

On the morning of the second day, Wikdinglieeth also known as Gatkuoth, left Kulang's house without being given food by Nyachom, because Kulang was already fed up with him for he had spent two days and two nights at his house. Gatkuoth became very disappointed and humiliated.

When Gatkuoth arrived at his house, he thought of revenge for what Kulang had done to him. Gatkuoth was one of the most vengeful in the land.

Three days later, Gatkuoth called his wife Nyaliem.

"Make a very delicious meal," he told his wife. "And I will slaughter a castrated he-goat because we will be going to the home of Kulang in Longtem near Toch town."

Gatkuoth's wife prepared everything including white wine as well. White wine is liked mostly by old men. The husband and his wife left at dawn towards Kulang's home.

When they finally arrived at Kulang's home, Gatkuoth went into the *Luak* where Kulang stayed but found him deep asleep and snoring. So, Gatkuoth told his wife to go and sit in the hut with Nyachom.

When Kulang woke up, he was so upset because he saw the same Gatkuoth, who supposed to have been gone, but ended sitting beside him in the same house. Gatkuoth greeted him but he wasn't interested in being greeted by the same guy.

Eventually he compromisingly replied and said: "*Maale Mi diit*", then he went silent for a while and didn't ask Gatkuoth back. The Nuer greeting-culture usually does not mean to hear about whatever may be actually troubling someone if someone does not feel well.

After a little while, Gatkuoth, called his wife and told her to bring some drinking water but Kulang angrily from his Gen, whispered to Gatkuoth: "My home has no water, why don't you guys carry with you some drinking water? My wife really suffers because of the continuous coming of the so-called visitors." Kulang said nakedly and turned his face away.

"*Gat-Toat*," Gatkuoth replied simply. "The water that I have requested is our water with my wife, it isn't your water."

Soon Gatkuoth's wife, Nyaliem, gave him some drinking water and after a short period of time, she brought the delicious food to her husband Gatkuoth, who ate alone without inviting Kulang.

Kulang sat up on his Gen trying to strike up a conversation when he saw Gatkuoth eat his food.

"Maa, may you tell me your nick name?" asked Kulang with a forced smile.

"Wikdinglieeth is my nick-name." Gatkuoth told him dryly, making it look as if he wanted to focus on his delicious food.

"Is it you whose name is known to all?" Kulang asked again beaming, thinking he would be told to come and eat. Gatkuoth answered him that he was the one if Kulang didn't know him. Kulang pretended as if he had not done bad thing to Gatkuoth before and Gatkuoth had intentionally come to insult him. Gatkuoth continued eating his delicious food alone despite all the interruptions from Kulang who wanted to eat with him.

When Gatkuoth finished his food; his wife came, took the dish and brought a pot full of white wine. Gatkuoth started to drink his white wine without inviting Kulang.

Meanwhile, Kulang persisted in his attempt to strike up a conversation. "*Maa*, Wikdinglieeth," he called desperately and hungrily. "Where do you come from?"

"I come from Chieng-Wanyaang-Kony." Gatkuoth answered him.

Finally, Kulang desperately and shamelessly asked Gatkuoth if he might have a sip of the wine but Gatkuoth paid a deaf ear to his despairing request.

The Nuer elders said: "Whatever gives insomnia or sleepless night to persons and prevents them from sleeping is their own making and no doubt that it comes within them."

Kulang was now victimized by his own making.

A story is told of a young man who was looking after his cattle in the forest. Accidentally he came across a skull of a human believed to have died many years before. The young man unknowingly kicked it as he satisfied himself after he looked at it for some few minutes.

"Why did you kick me?" The skull asked.

The young man became cold and surprised and ready to run but he maintained back his consciousness.

"What had killed you, Skull?" the young man asked it in shock.

"I died because of this 'red tongue' of mine?" replied the skull which was as white as piece of chalk.

Upon hearing that, the young man ran back to the village leaving his cattle alone in the bush. When he arrived, he informed all the villagers regarding the miracle that he had witnessed. The villagers didn't believe him and instead laughed at him. The young man didn't want to be called a liar for something that he had really witnessed. Therefore, the young man insisted and asked them to go with him on condition that he would be killed if the skull could not talk.

"I swear you will kill me if the skull doesn't talk" he promised.

Finally all people including the youth with no forgiveness accepted to go on the promise.

When they got to the point where the young man saw the skull, he was asked to make it talk.

The pride-engulfed young man came out and started to ask the skull. "What had killed you, Skull?" he asked.

There was no answer from the skull.

He repeated it several times "What had killed you, Skull?"

Unfortunately, the skull refused to talk. Now being that the young man had deceived them and brought the people all the way from the village to the bush, the elders who were with the angry youth could not safeguard the young man's life.

Suddenly the young man lay in the pool of blood after many spears from different youth entered his body. While the young man lay near the skull and was half-dead, the skull talked at last.

"You see my friend," said the white skull. "I said it clear that my red tongue had killed me. Now you are killed by your tongue"

All including those who kept their promises in killing him were surprised and became regretful after the skull had talked at last. But they couldn't do anything to bring back the poor young man to life.

Kulang was the cause of his own humiliation by Wikdinglieeth, similar to the story of that poor boy who was victimized by his own actions. A man is responsible for the effect of his actions. If the deed is based on goodness, it will churn out only goodness in the long run. If the deed has been wickedness, the outcome also tends to be wickedness.

Trying to please the man, Kulang tried to be as humane as possible with Gatkuoth:

"How are your kids, Wikdinglieeth?" Kulang asked. Gatkuoth replied that his kids were fine.

Finally, Gatkuoth asked Kulang and said, "Haven't you yet recognized me as we have been inside this *Luak*?"

"I have recognized you already, sir Wikdinglieeth." Kulang replied urgently.

Kulang became desperate for he saw the white wine but Gatkuoth didn't want to invite him because in Nuer culture one doesn't eat something he isn't invited to.

As the two were in a lengthy conversation, Kulang was slowly coming down unknowingly from his Gen. As he became near to Gatkuoth, his saliva dropped down with eyes popped out because he had taken a long period of time without drinking the white wine. Despite the fact that Gatkuoth saw Kulang's saliva on the ground as well as the desperation of Kulang, Gatkuoth didn't invite him.

When he finished his white wine alone, his wife came and took the pot. Meanwhile Gatkuoth became drunk and slept.

When he woke after a short rest, his wife brought him a very nice cooked fried he-goat's meat but he couldn't again invite Kulang, because he was so sad for he was asked before by Kulang, on whether he had cows, grain and other types of wealth.

As Gatkuoth, was eating, Kulang kept on interrupting by asking many questions so as to get his attention.

"*Maa Gat-Ruei Wuor!*" he said. "Maa owner of Dinglieth bull! Are men like Kony Nya-nguan, traditional head chief Kiy Wuor and his brother Ruei Wuor doing fine there in Paguir?" As he popped his eyes onto the food, his saliva dropped into the dish of meat which Gatkuoth was eating from.

Finally, Gatkuoth invited him to eat with him. Kulang smiled and talked to himself while eating: "If I hadn't treated this man bad before," he said. "He wouldn't have now denied me his delicious food and white wine. I have sinned because I did bad things to him before for I shall never repeat it. I must now answer my question; Wikdinglieeth has a lot of wealth".

When Gatkuoth finished, he said to Kulang,"Owner of Chot-nyanga bull I had to slaughter my fat he-goat simply because of what you had done to me in your house before. When I came to your house you asked me whether I had cows, grain or wealth and you turned the dish so that all milk could go to your side. Today I have come to show you that, I am a responsible man in his home that has a lot of wealth. That was the reason why I didn't call you to eat with me from the beginning. With this lesson, you won't again do it to any other person who may come to your house. Your behaviour is alien to the Nuer culture of hospitality. Selfishness is not good conduct you will have no friend and supporters even if war comes and you get wounded, no one will offer to take care of you because people will say let his dish and spoon take care of him. You Kulang! Your selfishness is beyond description and your name is known to all the communities of Lak and Thiäng including the neighbouring clans, so it is better to denounce self-centeredness. Now you have paid the price of the selfishness, for you normally eat alone. But why should your saliva drop down in the food of someone whom you had denied food before?"

Kulang helplessly replied, "Dear Wikdinglieeth, I am very sorry indeed for I haven't known you all this time that you are a son to Ruei Kerjiok. So you are a brother to my wife because Nyachom is a daughter of your clan Chieng-Gong-kiy… so forgive me."

Gatkuoth told him that, all the offcuts of his foods were inside the house; and they would remain with them. Gatkuoth with his wife Nyaliem, after a successful revenge mission, had to leave and waved goodbye to Kulang and his family.

The Nuer elders say, "An egotistical action hurts the doer."

There was once a selfish fox who invited a stork to a dinner at his home in a tree. That evening, the stork flew to the fox's home and knocked on the door with her long beak.

The fox opened the door and said, "Please come in and share my food." The stork was invited to sit down at the table. She was very hungry and the food smelled delicious!

The fox served soup in shallow bowls and he licked up all his soup very quick. However, the stork could not have any of it as the bowl was too shallow for her long beak. The poor stork just smiled politely and stayed hungry.

The selfish fox asked, "Stork, why haven't you taken your soup? Don't you like it?"

The stork replied, "it was very kind of you to invite me for dinner. Tomorrow evening, please join me for dinner at my home."

The next day when the fox arrived at the stork's house, he saw that they were also having soup for dinner. This time the soup was served in tall jugs. The stork drank the soup easily but the fox could not reach inside the tall jug.

"Fox, why haven't you taken your soup?" asked the stork in

revenge as she was asked before with the same question. "don't you like it?"

The fox could not answer as the questions were the same questions he had asked her before. This time it was the fox's turn to go hungry.

THIRTEEN

Kulang Faces off with Anyanya Fighters

At the inception of the Anyanya movement, the Anyanya soldiers under a Sgt. Major called Kuanen came to the home of Kulang. The Anyanya movement was the first Sudanese Civil War between the Africans of the country's Southern part against the Northern Arabs. Anyanya is a term in the Madi language which literally means 'snake venom'. The first and second Anyanya revolutions were conflicts from 1955 to the early 1980s that ended after the SPLA/M won the bush with its policies. Because there was no elections held. The Anyanya revolution was between the northern part of Sudan and the southern Sudan region that demanded an independent nation.

Sgt. Kuanen was the overall commander for the whole Fangak area. One hundred and forty soldiers arrived at the home of Kulang and were led by an officer called Wieh Duop Nyang. Kulang's home was located near the road. When Kulang saw a big number of soldiers arriving, he pretended as if he didn't see them because he knew they were the same soldiers who had slaughtered nine goats in his home before.

The soldiers did not know that Kulang was looking at them so one of the soldiers greeted him and said, "*Gat-Toat, Maale*" which means: 'How are you son of Toat?' a name out of respect in Nuer. When you call a person by his/her father it shows that you respect him/her.

"*Geet hook* (cattle looters), can your greeting be eaten?" Kulang said angrily.

Now the officer in charge again talked to him and said, "*Gat-bong-jaka, Maale!* Owner of the *Chot-nyanga* bull, *Maale! Turuk* has come to you, brother. We need something to eat."

Kulang didn't answer despite the admiration because he wanted only himself to be taken instead of his goats since he didn't want any of his goats to be taken. The soldiers knew very well that Kulang's *Luak* was full of goats.

Kulang finally answered, "Why do you insist on greeting me, is it because of my goats?"

Then he turned to the officer in charge wailing and crying sorrowfully "*WO! Ho Kuar! Ha Kuar Mi-diit*, my son! Help my poor goats who have been suffering from your sons for so long. My dog Ken Thiäng-dak and the goats themselves are my witnesses, ask them and they will tell you that I am right."

"Hi Ken-Thiäng-dak," he called his dog. "What are you doing there near your military-brothers? "

"Who is Ken-Thiäng-dak among us?" asked one of the soldiers angrily not knowing that Kulang's dog was behind them.

"My dog" He simply told them and pointing at his dog.

"Then where are its military-brothers?" asked another fuming soldier.

"Ask Ken-Thiäng-dak," Kulang said, "He will understand you. Brothers easily understand each other."

"Soldiers!" shouted the senior officer warning the soldiers who had nearly beaten Kulang. "Stop the war of words immediately!"

Luckily, the officer in charge agreed and called his adjutant to write a memo to Kulang, so that none of the soldiers in the area would touch his goats again. Kulang was handed a note protecting his goats from being eaten. Kulang became happy and took his Thom, called Nyachom with the guitar's sound because he feared beating and imprisonment from the soldiers. None of the soldiers knew that Kulang had called his wife as they had only heard the sound and soon Nyachom arrived. Kulang put the letter deep inside his goatskin pillow for he didn't want it to get lost.

A few days later, a different company of soldiers under Ruot Wich-luoth, who was responsible for the soldiers in the Lou-Nuer garrisons arrived and wanted food in the village. They finally reached Kulang's home and he told them that his goats had been suffering for so long and at last a senior commander wrote a memo to that effect. He happily handed the letter to the officer thinking that his goats would be left untouched.

Unfortunately, the officer torn the paper and ordered his soldiers to slaughter one of the goats. Kulang cried and had to run to Nyachom and blame it on her.

"Nyachom, Nyachom," he called in despair. "It is your writer who wrote that my goats should be slaughtered."

He then turned to the soldiers with heavy face. "You, brothers of Ken-Thiäng-dak and Guichi Ha Ngu, I thought your being in

bushes is to free us but now you are oppressing us instead. Why would you slaughter my Chot-rola-ox when a memo is written to protect it? I thought your messages were one like harpoons when one of your comrades wrote it for me. Now your success will take a long period of time because you oppose, betray and backstab each other. And you fight the Arab with anger not courage."

A year or so later the official opening of Toch town was announced. Before Toch was discovered and opened up for navigation, it was named 'Longtime' by the colonial explorers, because it used to take a long time for them to reach it from Fangak. The natives, after difficulty in pronouncing it, later pronounced it 'Longteem'. It was in the year 1963 when Toch was publicly opened up by the Inspector General called Moses Chuol Juch. When it was officially opened, there were soldiers under a veteran called Mathot Chang, and Majuol Ruei Wuor, who arrived at Longteem and settled at Kulang's home waiting till the morning in order to build their base in the newly opened administrative area.

That development infuriated Kulang very much. He tried different styles to let them go but to no avail as the soldiers used force in everything. Kulang knew it very well that the stopover of the soldiers at his home means slaughtering of either his goats or cows. So he left for a walk in the neighbourhood.

A minute later he returned to find that the soldiers had, without permission, selected his grey cow for slaughtering. "This cow of mine is not 'boot'." he said irately. "It is *liach*." But the soldiers paid deaf ears to Kulang's excuse and instead went on in slaughtering the cow. 'Boot' is a cow which doesn't produce calves and '*liach*' is a pregnant cow.

"Now that you have slaughtered your mother-cow." he angrily told them. "Have you found an Arab inside?"

FOURTEEN

Kulang's Greed and Insanity

Because the primary occupation of the Nuer people is raising livestock, they value the cattle more than anything. In the past, the people had no idea of their age because they had no education and had no radios and televisions. Feeding and taking care of the cattle was the first priority as wealth and riches were often measured by the size of the cattle herd. Fame, the next most important thing, was also brought by the more cattle one had, as well as bravery in a given sectional or tribal fight.

The coefficients in a Nuer herder's life haven't changed much in generations as villagers still live life as they did in the past. According to the Nuer culture, boys are in charge of the herding of livestock. At a young age, they take care of the goats, sheep, and calves, which are normally herded together close to the village or homes. As the boys grow up, they graduate to herding cattle and not sheep, goats and calves as they used to do when young. The herd boys often carry spears and other traditional weapons with them to protect themselves as well as their cattle from external threats be it animals or humans. They closely monitor their cattle to avoid losing cattle to cattle looters or animals attack. The decision of the grazing or pasture areas for the cattle is decided by the elders. Boys only implement the orders from the elders.

There was this day, during the rainy season, some young herders came and grazed their cattle not far from the *Luak* of Kulang as per the directives of their fathers because of the good grasslands around Kulang's home. Soon the clouds gathered and the rain could be smelt by both the boys and the cows although the rain has no scent. Now it was going to rain and there was only Kulang's home near to the young boys. All except one of them knew Kulang very well and that he did not always cooperate with people. The young boys decided not to run to take shelter in Kulang's *Luak* when it was raining to avoid humiliation. But one of them decided otherwise to take shelter at Kulang's *Luak* during the rain.

"Is he not a human? Why would we stay in the rain when there is a home nearby?" the boy said, opposing the decision taken by the majority in refusing to go to Kulang's home. A few minutes later, there was a little drizzling rain which was a signal that heavy rain was coming ahead. The other boys decided to stay in the rain while the one who disagreed with them before decided to run to Kulang's *Luak*.

When the young man arrived inside the *Luak*, he found Kulang's food was ready. When he saw the boy about his sons' age with him inside the *Luak*, Kulang employed tactfulness to chase the young boy away. He gave a forced smile and promised that the young boy could eat with him on the condition that the boy should act as if a husband and his wife were having sexual intimacy, while the door was shut so that when the other boys attempted to come to enter they would not do so out of respect.

"Young man," he began, with a falsified seriousness. "Please start moaning and sighing now as we are eating and the door is closed so that when those hungry boys try to come in I shall tell them that I am with my wife producing kids."

Upon hearing this, the guy angrily jumped to his feet and ran back because anything of that subject (for a man to pretend to be like a woman simply for a reward), is an abomination and taboo not only in Naath culture but in African traditional society as a whole. Kulang knew it very well that one can lead a Nuer-man to a meeting place, but he can't change his thoughts which was why he came up with an impossible demand and request against the will and dignity of the young man because he knew the gentleman would not accept the request.

Upon hearing this, the guy angrily jumped to his feet and ran back.

FIFTEEN

Kulang Discovers the Telephone

In 1954, the colonial district commissioner sent Kulang to jail in Fangak, after he refused to pay the government's taxes. Kulang couldn't eat well in jail due to the nature and treatment of the prisoners in terms of the accommodation and feeding. Kulang became very weak and thin in just few days inside the detention center because he couldn't get enough food as he used to get in his home.

The officer in charge of the prisoners approached him one evening after coming from work: "Why have you become so thin and weak so soon like this?" asked the officer.

Kulang replied that the food he was always given was not only little but bad.

"A person in jail neither eats enough food nor good food." said the officer in charge with smile on his face

"Then expect my death in two days," said Kulang desperately and sadly. "But what worries me is to die when my dear wife is not there."

The officer was going to talk when Kulang continued talking more and more.

"Can you let Nyachom come," he continued. "So that I rest in peace while she is here."

The officer in charge was moved in pity with him and promised to let Nyachom come to him. The officer asked what Nyachom could also bring if she were to come.

"Well," Kulang said with a smile on his face. "Cow's butter, fried meat, castrated he-goat, food in a gourd, cooked millet with beans…"

The officer's paper got full with Kulang's uncountable demands.

"But how will my things and Nyachom come?" he asked again. "Do not worry we have a telephone and a car." the officer assured. "Nyachom and all your demands will reach you soon."

The police authority in charge decided to bring Kulang's wife to the detention centre as Kulang's body was slowly fading away due to hunger and burnout. They phoned their headquarters near the place where Nyachom resided so that she was brought to cook for her hunger-dying husband. After an order from the top authority, the police station in charge there sent their junior comrades to go to the area where Nyachom lived.

Nyachom was told by the police authority that she was needed by her husband at the police post in order to cook for him. When Kulang physically saw Nyachom with his demands, he wondered in happiness and questioned how his wife could come to him on time. He was told that Nyachom was called on the phone.

Upon hearing that, he said, "I must buy this phone from you. It deserves to be my friend in this world."

The officer in charge told him that government property wasn't for sale.

"Okay, does it have daughters?" he said. "So that I marry the phone's daughter when I am released from the jail because someone who can quickly and easily bring to me my dear wife deserves something good like a marriage relationship."

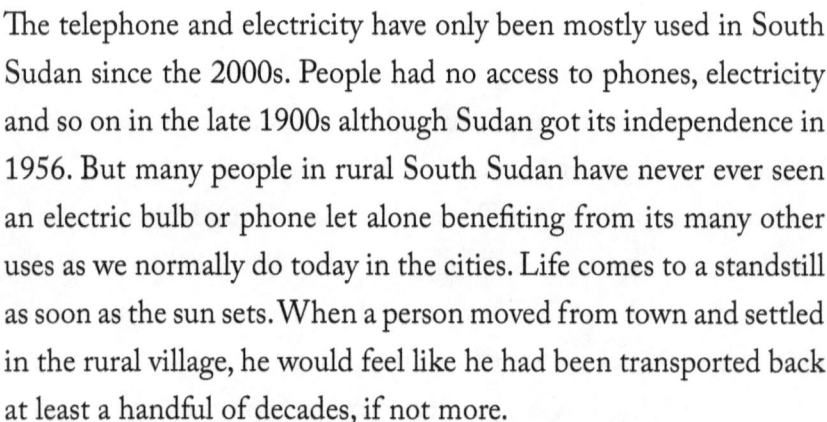

The telephone and electricity have only been mostly used in South Sudan since the 2000s. People had no access to phones, electricity and so on in the late 1900s although Sudan got its independence in 1956. But many people in rural South Sudan have never ever seen an electric bulb or phone let alone benefiting from its many other uses as we normally do today in the cities. Life comes to a standstill as soon as the sun sets. When a person moved from town and settled in the rural village, he would feel like he had been transported back at least a handful of decades, if not more.

Food is to be cooked before it gets dark or else people would sleep without food and children are forced to go inside their mosquito nets after a short play. Folktales whose main characters are animals are always told while people lay down on their sleeping mates with closed eyes as nothing can be seen in darkness. Young people and women are not allowed to go further at night for fear of wild animals and beasts.

Kulang Discovers the Telephone

The Colonial District Commissioner sent Kulang to jail in Fangak after he refused to pay the Government's taxes.

SIXTEEN

Kulang Denies his Nephew

One day, Kulang's nephew came to him at his home. Upon arrival, he greeted his uncle respectfully by giving his head to Kulang as per the tradition. Children give their head instead of hands to the elderly people to spit on with some saliva as greeting with respect.

Now the boy did as per the culture but his uncle acted as if he didn't see or know him because the nephew arrived at a time when Kulang was served with food.

"Uncle, it is me the son of your sister Nya-Toat." the boy said while bending down giving his head to Kulang for greeting.

"Toat of which year?" Kulang replied. "This year or last year?" he asked such a ridiculous question so that he discouraged his nephew. Kulang's father's name 'Toat' means autumn or rainy season that was why he asked his nephew whether he meant this year's autumn or the autumn of the previous year. He made that trick so that he could jump to either of this year or last year based on his nephew's answer because he didn't want to have him related at all during the meal.

The boy after the words of Kulang thought that his uncle had eventually forgotten him as a result of old age. "Uncle, you are right for not recognizing me because you have grown old and human

Kulang Denies his Nephew

Uncle, it is me the son of your sister, Nya-Toat.

sight goes down with old age, that is why you don't recognize me." said the boy.

"No, no boy," Kulang replied. "Not because of eye problem as you falsely said. Even if I was born today or you were put into my eyes, I wouldn't recognize you totally, just move."

From there his nephew returned to their home very disappointed because he was thwarted by his uncle. It was easier to wake up someone who pretended to sleep than to try to convince Kulang.

Greed sometimes takes away people's belongings as there was once a man who liked everything to be his own. He could not share his belongings with anyone, not even his friends or the poor.

One day, the man lost thirty gold coins. He searched for it but to no avail. He finally went to his friend's house and told him how he had lost his gold coins. His friend was a kind man.

As his friend's daughter was coming home from an errand, she found thirty gold coins. When she arrived home, she told her father what she had found. The girl's father told her that the gold coins belonged to his friend and he sent for him. When the greedy man arrived, he told him how his daughter had found his thirty gold coins and handed them to him. After counting the gold coins, the greedy man said that ten of them were missing and had been taken by the girl as he had forty gold coins. He further commented that he would recover the remaining amount from him. But the girl's father refused.

The greedy man left the gold coins and went to the court and informed the judge there about what had taken place between him and the girl's father.

The judge sent for the girl and her father, and when they arrived, the judge asked the girl of how many coins she had found. She replied that she had only found thirty gold coins. The judge then turned to the greedy man and asked him of how many coins he had lost. The greedy man replied that he had lost forty gold coins.

The judge then told the greedy man that the gold coins did not belong to him because the girl found thirty and not forty as he claimed to have lost and then told the girl to take the gold coins and that if anybody was looking for them he would send for her. The judge told the selfish man that if anybody reported that they had found forty gold coins he would send for him. It was then that the man confessed that he had lied and that he lost thirty gold coins but the judge did not listen to him.

SEVENTEEN

Kulang and Food Security

Nyachom was preparing a very delicious meal while her husband, Kulang, was keenly monitoring from a short distance with all his attention. The cooking was always done in three earthen stones around the vast built place called buur, molded and simply left in the sun to dry. Most of the cooking utensils were made of clay.

While the food was being cooked by Nyachom, he accidentally saw one of the burning firewood under the pot on fire and warned his wife regarding the danger.

"Nyachom," he cried, pointing at the fire logs. "Look at that fire log, it is unstable now for it may touch this firewood which may also touch that firewood that may go and touch the other big burning log which could also touch and twist the cooking pot and may lead the pot to collapse."

Kulang always followed every step during cooking. He knew very well about food security. Therefore, Nyachom was expected to put her husband's warning into highest consideration for the food to be safe.

After a short time when Nyachom put down the food, she gave her kids food while Kulang was expecting to be served first.

Look at that fire log, it is unstable now for it may touch this firewood.

"Nyachom! Nyachom Loang!" he called furiously. "I have never even in a minute thought you would betray me until today. How could you belittle your own husband by serving only the kids first leaving him hungry? Whom have you known first between your kids and me? Where were your kids when I was looking for you long ago? Don't you know that they have recently joined our life from nowhere? Nyacohm, you are a traitor." Nyachom, in fear, was nodding her head in approval of Kulang's speech.

Kulang blamed his wife for betraying him as he was the person who took good care of the food on the fire.

"Had it not been me monitoring the food," he continued. "It would have poured down." He talked heatedly to his wife claiming to have been betrayed badly by giving the kids first leaving him as a lesser priority.

A related story is told about the crane and the snake. In a forest close to the riverbank, lived a crane and his wife. They were very unhappy because every time the wife laid eggs in their nest, a big black cobra that lived in a hollow in the tree, would eat them up.

The crane had a friend, the crab. He went to his friend to seek some advice regarding the matter.

When the crane arrived at his friend's house, he shared his misery with him. "I feel so hopeless because that sneaking thief has always been eating our eggs." complained the crane angrily.

"Do not worry," said the crab comfortingly. "You need not to be hopeless when you have a friend like me. We will come up with a solution."

The crab sat to think of a plan. Suddenly he jumped and rushed to the crane. "Friend, I have a wonderful plan." said the crab and whispered something into the crane's ear. The crane flew back to his nest and told his wife all about the crab's plan. He was very excited.

"Are you sure this will work?" asked the wife. "I hope we are not making a mistake. Think twice before going ahead with the plan."

But the crane was eager to try out the plan. The crane flew down to the riverbank and began to fish. He caught several little fish and went down to the hole in which a mongoose lived. He dropped a fish at the mouth of the hole. Then he took another fish and dropped it a little further away from the first one. Repeating this, he made a trail of fish leading to the tree where his nest was.

The mongoose smelt the fish and came out of the hole. "Ah, a fish!" exclaimed the mongoose joyfully and quickly ate it up. He then followed the trail of fish. As he neared the tree where the cranes and the snake lived, the trail ended.

Finding no more fish, he looked around. Suddenly he came across the black cobra at the foot of the tree. Seeing the mongoose, the cobra fought for his life. Both fought for a long time and in the end the mongoose killed the snake. The cranes who were watching the fight from their nest sighed with relief. The next day the mongoose began to follow the same trail hoping to find more food. When he came to the tree where the trail ended, he decided to climb the tree in search of food.

The cranes that were away at the riverbank returned to find the mongoose climbing down the tree. On looking in their nest, they discovered that this time, the mongoose had eaten up all their eggs.

"Alas! We got rid of one enemy only to find another," said the crane to his wife.

Finally, Nyachom in fright withdrew the kids' plate and served Kulang first for her safety.

"Yes," he smiled. "This is what we call true love. I could not monitor the food only to be the last to be served. Lovers serve themselves first before third persons. If I am not better than the kids to you, but you are better than the kids to me."

EIGHTEEN

The Visitor from Far

It was a stifling summer day, the air was muggy and the leaves of the trees hanged down and people used 'Kot', made of sisal leaves to help them relieve nature's heat and distress. Kulang was sitting inside his *Luak* when he glared for a long time and finally saw something from far.

As Nyachom was taking food to him inside the *Luak*, they met at the door-way and he stopped her with a loud voice of warning and instructed her to take the food back because he saw someone at a distance putting '*Nok*' (A bird's feather) on his head and seemed to be coming home.

"Stop!" he cried. "I see a coming human figure there, my dear wife!"

Nyachom turned and looked at the person who was far away and discovered the person was going.

"I see it too." Nyachom confirmed. "But it is a going figure."

"No, he is coming." he said.

The two couples began to argue on whether the person was coming or going. Nyachom wanted her husband to eat because she knew actually that no one was coming but Kulang feared that the person would surprisingly reach home and might eat with him.

Kulang was sitting inside his Luak *when he glared for a long time and finally saw something from far.*

Kulang insisted that the person was coming but Nyachom opposed by saying he was going.

"Mother of my kids, he is coming!"

"He is going, father of my kids?"

"He is really coming!"

"No, he is going please."

The debate continued again, again and again until the person disappeared and Kulang peacefully and happily enjoyed his food.

Kulang hated visitors in his life. He expected them to work in their gardens instead of visiting different homes. He feared visitors would not only eat his food but bring bad omens to the already peaceful family.

A story was told of one of the visitors who brought misery to a peaceful family at that time. The visitor after arriving was served with food and drinks.

A baby was sleeping near the visitor as he was eating his food. And there was a calf, dog and a chicken not far away from where the baby was sleeping. The dog was looking at the visitor as it wanted food. Because the Nuer people don't like someone who doesn't give food to pets, the man gave a portion of little food to the dog that was badly looking at him.

When the chicken saw that the dog was given food, it ran in order to snip it but the dog was ready for the defensive fight. The dog frightened the chicken fiercely and chased it away. The chicken ran away for its life and jumped on the back of the calf which was sitting peacefully.

Unfortunately, the calf got startled for the chicken that sat at its back. Trying to let down what was on it back; the calf jumped over the child and killed the child instantly.

All this was in Kulang's calculations as it was always difficult to point at who to blame between the woman, the visitor, the dog, the chicken, the calf, the child and the death. You, the reader, can now judge fairly!

It would have been a disaster to Kulang if the man had really come to see Kulang and he either didn't want to eat with him or didn't want any problem like the strange story of one of the visitors. Perhaps Kulang was preventing potential problems with the visitors rather than solving them later as it is said 'Prevention is better than cure.'

If we become focused on gathering more wealth, we become focused and driven by egocentricity and we will never be content. Egocentricity itself opens the door to other sins and we find ourselves falling farther from God and what He has for our precious lives. We must be careful to protect our hearts and minds against egocentrism and to practice contentment. We must be generous in giving and sharing.

NINETEEN

Kulang in the Forest of Dates

The dates are the fruit of the date palm mostly grown in the northern part of the Sudan. It is a berry of golden yellow colour or reddish-brown when ripe. Its meat is soft, aromatic and very sweet, with an elongated shaped stone inside it and a longitudinal furrow. This kind of tree doesn't grow in South Sudan. The Lalob tree (Balanites agyptiaca which is believed to be a member of either Zygophyllaceae or the Balanitaceae) grows in South Sudan.

It was a quite cold day when a stranger from another village surprised Kulang in his farmstead. Kulang's heart beat fast for he thought the man was going to seek lodging.

Alas, the stranger was a trader who had just arrived from Dongola in order to sell his goods in the countryside. The man had a heavy sack on his head and it was full of dates. When he put down his heavy sack, he gave Kulang some dates to taste. When Kulang tasted the dates, he found that they were very sweet.

He then joyfully asked the man about the name of the fruit: "What do you call this fruit, Gatgualen?" he asked.

"They are called dates and they grow in bushes and deserts." he was told.

Kulang also asked if they grew like beans nevertheless, he was told that they grew like the rest of trees in bushes.

Then he lamented in despair and said, "Wo! I wish I could get lost in the forest of dates for the rest of my life so that it can be my main food."

"God divided things unfairly, why would He give these sweet dates to Arabs alone and gave us the Lalob fruits with bad taste?" he was very angry as he talked.

After he was told exactly the land where dates grew, he decided to go there in person. He sold a cow and waited to go with some traders who were going to bring goods back from the North.

On one summer season day Kulang and his companions left Fangak for Dongola. It took them two months to reach the town of Dongola as they were travelling on foot. Dongola is a town whose forest had a lot of the Arecaceae Palm trees that bore dates. Kulang and his travelling companions arrived and were warmly welcomed.

All of the travellers sat on beds that were given to them by the Shiekh of the town except Kulang who went and sat under a nearby date-palm tree. Kulang's move didn't only surprise the Shiekh but his companions too.

The people talked among themselves as to why one of their visitors declined to sit comfortably on the given beds and instead prepared the dirty ground beneath a tree. They finally decided to send the oldest man in the town to go and ask him to return to join his companions.

"Good evening young man." he was greeted.

Wo! I wish I could get lost in the Forest of Dates for the rest of my life so that it can be my main food.

"Good evening to you, sir." he cheerfully replied, but there was no bad face on him to show that he had objections.

"First of all, I would like to welcome you to Dongola." the old man began. "I have come with two things in mind to you here; to take you back and sit where people are and to know what has exactly disappointed you to come here and sit on the ground."

"I have no problem with anybody and I will never have problem with anyone in a town like Dongola for the rest of my life." Kulang said.

"Then," said the old man, "tell us why you have sat lonely here."

"One sits under the shade of what he comes for." Kulang simply replied. "I have come along the way from my land purposely for this tree. It would be a betrayal if I didn't sit under its shade because it's the object of my coming."

Lastly the old man returned and reported the development to the people who were eagerly waiting to know what had isolated Kulang. Kulang refused to join the people in the house and had to continue sleeping under the tree for some days until he bought some sacks of dates.

Kulang admired the town calling it 'Heavenly town' because of its sweet dates. He at first decided not to return to his land for the rest of his life to continue eating dates in Dongola but he later changed his mind when he remembered his wife, children and the strong men of his land.

He ate as much dates as he could. When he finished eating the dates he wailed:

"Oh! Is this the Khartoum date that I used to hear?" he said sharply. "This place would make a good place for grazing cattle. If it were one of the forests in South Sudan where boys graze cattle at, I would not allow any boy to it. I would instead daily take care of the grazing cattle till the end of the world.

"Instead of staying here forever, I must make South Sudan to be Dongola by growing the tree there. I am tired of Lalob trees for so long."

Kulang finally left Dongola and returned to Toch with handful sacks of dates which no one could afford to carry from Dongola to Fangak.

TWENTY

Kulang Declares Rebellion

The Anyanya soldiers came to the home of Kulang and wanted a goat for their lunch. They selected a very fat goat. This angered Kulang who said they should not take it, instead, he pointed at a different goat and the soldiers refused because it was thin and skinny and could not satisfy them.

They began to argue over who to surrender between the soldiers and himself.

When Kulang knew that the soldiers wouldn't give-up, he smiled and said to his kids: "Let them take that fat goat which is pregnant with an Arab child." Kulang said that because he knew that the enemies of the soldiers were Arabs.

This made the soldiers leave the goat in question and instead, took the skinny goat which he had suggested to them at first. "*Ngoth ka baaw,*" he joked.

A year later, they came back again wanting another meal from his home but they didn't find him at home. They instead, selected a goat among the goats and told the kids that they would be back when Kulang arrived because they were going to different homes to search for more food since the former veterans were depending on the civil population for accommodation during their fight against the Arabs' regime.

When Kulang came home, he was told about the goat which was chosen among the goats and was also told by his kids that the soldiers would come back to take it. When he heard that, he took the selected goat and went some meters away from his home. Kulang reached a small bush behind his compound and it was this bush where he slaughtered the goat, and roasted it claiming to have rebelled and joined the bushes as a liberator against the oppressors. When the soldiers arrived, they found him eating the meat of the goat that they had selected.

"Look," Kulang whispered, and the handful of soldiers surrounded him. "I have from today officially rebelled, because rebellion is very easy. Someone just lazily leaves his home to loot others. Fortunately, Kulang is a courageous rebel who doesn't loot other people's property like you. I am a smart rebel who loots his own belongings."

"Many soldiers are brave when the enemy is far." he continued insulting the surprised soldiers. "I only trust the brave soldiers near the enemy. Struggle continues." he concluded as he was eating the meat and he was inwardly mocking the soldiers.

Kulang's trick surprised the soldiers because he was the only person who didn't fear them as many frightening stories between soldiers and the civil population had occurred. There was once a man whose blanket was stolen by one of the soldiers and he could see the soldier carrying the blanket with him. Fearfully the man asked the soldier: "My son, didn't my blanket fall on your shoulder?".

But the soldier couldn't answer him as he was still going ahead. Another story said that there was a man who heard a voice of distress in an open toilet in his garden but he didn't know it was a soldier. He thought it was an ordinary person and not a soldier. The people used the dry and open defecation outside the open environment. They did so because they had no toilets or latrines as it was an abomination for earth to be dug for what they simply believed to be 'defecation'. Earth was dug only to bury the dead people.

He slaughtered the goat and roasted it, claiming to have rebelled and joined the bushes as a liberator against the oppressors.

Therefore, the man in an angry voice said, "Who is that idiot defecating in my garden?" When he saw him in uniform and gun, he had nearly run out of his skin. He instead fearfully apologized and said, "Ha, sorry, soldier, my dear son. Enjoy and be free even if you want to defecate in my house."

With the man's pleasing words, the soldier left without beating the owner of the garden that he was defecating in.

Finally, the soldiers left Kulang who didn't fear them at all. Kulang, after finishing the meat of the goat alone, left for his home after what he considered to be a tactical retreat against the soldiers.

TWENTY-ONE

Kulang Sues his Dog

One day, a very delicious meal mixed with well-prepared beef was prepared for Kulang in his *Luak* by his wife Nyachom. His dog, Guichi Ha Ngu, followed her because it wanted to be given some food.

When Kulang knew that the dog wanted some part of his food with delicious delicacy, he moved up to his Gen (a traditionally made papyrus bed high in the middle of the *Luak* with the fire bank underneath), so that the dog couldn't have access to him. Unfortunately, the eyes of the dog were fixated on him and he tried to move back to avoid eye contact with the dog which was too determined to get a bit at all costs.

Kulang, upon seeing the dog's seriousness, moved to the other side of his Gen thinking that the dog would not be able to stare at his delicious food. Unfortunately, the dog intentionally moved backward by another suitable distance and so he was able to stare at Kulang's food again. Pissed off, Kulang moved to the far end of his Gen, but the dog moved backward by an equal distance. This went on for a while and every time Kulang lifted his food to change position, the dog would shift his position too by an equal distance.

At the end Kulang ran out of space and fell off on his back. His face ended up in the dish as the dish turned upside down, luckily, the dish with the food in it overturned on his chest.

He lamented: "*Wo*, devil, devil! You think you will taste my food," he said, "I will never give you. Hopeless idiot, who has no home, who loves and makes fornication with his sisters, Torn-mouth guy who puts his hands down to look like legs so that he doesn't work and

Torn-mouth guy who puts his hands down to look like legs so that he doesn't work and deceives people that he has no hands.

deceives people that he has no hands. I am done with you, idiot. Why do you love your sisters? Yet they can be married and you can get cows that can give you milk just as my sisters were married, Mr. Asshole. Today our relationship has ended, so if you have anything that belongs to you, take it. You cannot disturb me always simply because of the dead animals' skulls that you always bring. If you think you are right, let us go to the court. Here take the money, go to the head chief and call me so that we sit in the court, idiot Guichi Ha Ngu?".

There was a superstition in Nuer about the origin of the dog and that might be the reason why Kulang took it so seriously as to insult the dog.

That story about the first dog goes like this: once upon a time, a dog used to be a wealthy creature. Because of pride the dog thought its wealth would never end.

A human being was burning grass that he had removed from his garden when the dog approached and challenged him in a contest.

"Set my barns on fire if you are a man enough," said the dog. The story has it that the human set fire on the dog's barns and as a result, all the dog's resources got burned completely. A year later, after the dog's wealth completely gone, there was a tough famine on earth as survival was too hard for all the creatures. The dog knew what to do after he became weak of hunger.

He visited his uncle, the fox, who he thought would help him with some advice on survival as the dog became hopeless.

"Hello, Uncle," he waved to the fox.

He was waved back warmly as you know the relation between an uncle and a nephew.

"I have come to seek advice from you because famine has got the best of me." He began. "For that reason, I want your advice as I have already decided to join the human in his land because he has everything."

His uncle fox was believed to be the toughest clairvoyant on earth. Now he brought his magic stones to see the dog's future fate.

"Hi Gatnyieri," cried the fox. "The human will castrate you, will cut your ears. Pitch your food on ground. Beat you, tie you with rope. They will say all sorts of bad words against you if you speak. Better turn to be hearing-impaired for your safety."

"Thank you, uncle," the dog expressed gratitude to him. "But what shall I do?"

"Better bear all that I have told you than dying of hunger since twisting is better than breaking." said the fox. From that time the dog has lived with human with all that the fox had said.

Kulang might have been implementing the fox's conditions on dogs when he insulted the dog badly. And you, the reader, might have for a certain time implemented some if not all of the fox's words against dogs. Throwing stones at dogs, beating and insulting them. Finally, Nyachom came to his rescue and the food was safe.

TWENTY-TWO

Death Accusation

A young man came to the hut of Kulang and found out he was being served with food. Kulang thought for a while on how to ensure that the young man couldn't get food.

He greeted the young man and asked him if he respected elderly people or not. The boy assured him that it was his duty to respect elderly people. Kulang told him that it was in the culture for the people to chat first before they could eat any meal. But he was in fact trying to find a reason to get rid of the young man.

"Young man," he called with smirk in his face. "You know I want to talk to you passively now but I fear you may have an argument since you, the generation of nowadays, argue and oppose elders."

The boy replied and said, "No uncle, don't fear. Let's just make conversation because I respect elderly people. I will never make an argument with you."

"Are you sure that you won't oppose me later?"

"Yes I am."

"Well," Kulang began by asking a ridiculous question. "Are you the boy who was killed last time during the fight?"

The boy was surprised and frightened by such a question from Kulang, but nevertheless, gave a positive reply.

Kulang told him that it was in the culture for the people to chat first before eating any meal.

"No uncle," replied the boy "That was not me. That might be a different person."

"Young man, I saw you myself dead in front of all the people." Kulang angrily whispered, pointing at the little boy. "Why do you deny the fact?"

My home is not a cemetery for dead people.

The boy again refuted, trying to convince Kulang that he was not the one.

"Uncle, if I had been killed in the fight," he said logically. "I would not be talking to you now. That is the evidence that the person you found dead was a different person and not me."

Kulang heatedly lamented: "Wo! Boy! Didn't I tell you that you would make an endless argument with me? I dislike someone who died and pretend to live. Who do you want to fool, stupid boy? Go away and leave me alone. You have just told me that you respect your elderly people. Where is the respect here, idiot?"

From there Kulang stretched out his hand, picked up his fighting stick, gave the boy some lashes and the boy resisted by running away for his safety.

"My home is not a cemetery for dead people." cried Kulang, while running after the boy. "I must return you to your grave today, dead boy."

The young man ended up leaving Kulang's home and went straight to his village, not expecting what had just transpired. The young man eventually concluded that it was because Kulang wanted to eat alone and did not want anybody around to look at him while eating.

TWENTY-THREE

Kulang Finds his Like

Early one morning, Kulang prepared to leave on a visit to a village that he had never been to all his life. He started his journey to that village which was very far away from his home area of Toch. He reached a certain home along the road and saw a man called Ganyang, who was believed to be selfish.

Ganyang first had to be tied at both hands and legs by the strongest men of his village simply because of his appetite for food as he would disturb his wives had he not been tied before the food got ready. If he was not tied well, he would jump and harm himself with hot soup. Every time his wives wanted to cook, they would first inform the village's strongest men to tie him up so that they could cook without interruption and he would get untied when food was ready.

The Nuer people say, 'The hyenas that laugh are less than the hyenas that do not laugh.'

When Kulang arrived in Ganyang's home, he was suddenly surprised by three strong men who lifted the owner of the home to his feet. The man offered little resistance as the men tied him up tightly in a sisal rope and handcuffed his hands and legs. None of Ganyang's captors were his enemies but his best friends.

That scenario surprised Kulang, who immediately went back and called together the people in his village regarding the miracle he saw. "Listen," he shouted. "Last week, I had a journey somewhere around the world. Let me tell you the miracle that I saw with my two eyes."

He cleared his throat for a clear voice to come out as he was ready to start the story. He thought before he left his village that there was no village other than his own and its surroundings. The world to Kulang centered on his village and its surroundings, and a two to three days walk would mean reaching the far end of the earth.

"I have seen a selfish man in one of the villages," Kulang started to tell his story. "The man was tied by the whole village when his wives wanted to start cooking, for if he wasn't tied well, he would burn himself and the people around him. He would be untied only when food was ready and cold." Kulang was emotionally narrating the story such that people could stop calling him selfish. He wanted to be considered a good man who ate and shared with people when the opposite was true of him. Kulang didn't know that he was an avaricious man as far as food was concerned.

Kulang did not know that the world was very big and contained all types of people.

Stories of people tougher than him were told. There was a certain man who, after only two days without food, went to the bush to find food. He tried but in vain. At last he had thought to go fishing in the river.

Luckily, he found a small fish that could not relieve his starvation, so he decided to make soup out of it. After he knew the soup was ready and there was no food, he went toward a nearby anthill, washed his hands and ate up the anthill with the soup of a fish that he had cooked. The man died instantly after he had filled his stomach with the mud of the anthill that did not give chance to his stomach to digest it.

If he was not tied well, he would jump and harm himself with hot soup.

TWENTY-FOUR

The Cold War

Kulang sent for his brother in-law and asked him to bring him sisal leaves which were used for knitting the cattle' robes, building grass-thatched houses, as well as binding tall tree branches in order to make fences and huts as traditional African builders normally do. Nuer people normally make fences for their homes to feel secure and to give it a definite border. When his brother in-law received the message, he immediately left their home for the bush to cut sisal leaves as requested by his in-law, Kulang.

Marriage relationships are highly respected and cherished across the Nuer land. Both mother in-law and father in-law aren't allowed to eat or drink in their daughter's home whatsoever the circumstance may be, and they aren't allowed to greet by shaking hands with their daughter's husband. When one of them dies, the son of their daughter doesn't entomb or bury them but instead a stranger is hired if the biological sons or immediate relatives aren't available to bury the dead, for if the daughter's sons do so, it is believed bad omens will occur to them as it is an ancestral custom. Sisters-in-law and brothers-in-law are allowed to stay, eat or drink in their sister's home.

Normally if the in-laws asked for help, it would be done as a matter of priority as soon as possible. That was the reason why

Kulang's brother in-law had to respond immediately because marriage relationships are respected in the Nuer tradition.

Kulang's in-law cut enough sisal leaves and came to his sister's home. Upon arrival, he was warmly welcomed by his sister as well as his sister's husband, Kulang. The in-law then ate happily with Kulang, with smile on their faces for the first two days. But when the in-law was willing to spend some more days in the house beyond Kulang's expectations, he became angry.

Kulang thought a trick. "I must do a trick to let this idiot go." he thought loudly to himself.

He tried all the tactics in order for his in-law to leave the house but all failed. The in-law couldn't go because he believed that it was his right to spend some days in his sister's house where he brought sisal leaves for building. Lastly, Kulang decided to break his silence through his Thom that he always used for sending important and urgent cases to his wife. Thom was the only option remaining after he failed several times with other tactics, including bad body language, he had used in trying to chase him away.

"*Ding ding*," went on the sound of the Thom. "*Nin wal par ken ke run wal, nyame Nyachom luek damuor bikor tuok wale.*" Which literally means: 'Ten days have now become like ten years. Nyachom please advise your brother, war is in the corner.' His wife and the brother in-law heard and understood all the words through the sound of the guitar, but to the surprise of Kulang, his brother in-law had a *Thom* and knew how to use it very well.

'*Ding ding*', went on the imitation and beating of the Thom by Kulang's brother in-law. '*Me lar e jin i nongni kaan, nin dial ba ke nin*

To the surprise of Kulang, his brother-in-law had a Thom and knew how to use it very well.

chiengdu.' Which means: 'It was you who said I should bring sisal leaves, for that matter I will spend more days here.'

The two had never verbally attacked each other instead they used the Thom until the in-law left after few days. Finally, Kulang became happy to continue eating alone without any one on the other side of the dish.

TWENTY-FIVE

Kulang Sells his Cattle

Between 1961 and 1972, there was a severe flood that affected most parts of the then southern Sudan region as the rainfall was very heavy during that time. Many people left their homes for higher grounds, providing guiding principles on where to build their homes, where to travel, where to take their livestock, and what to do during that natural hazardous emergency. The Nuer elders say, 'It is possible for the cows to be broken up into pieces and stored in the shed during the worse times.'

Kulang was now going to apply the Nuer elders' proverb after he had realized before many people that the forthcoming floods were going to be very serious indeed and were likely to overwhelm the local cattle population.

One cold morning, Kulang called his son, Chamkuan, regarding the danger of the flood.

"Chamkuan, my son," he began. "Now cattle die like coconut fruits and people die like flies on the daily basis from this dangerous flood. Because of that, we must now pack our cattle in boxes for their safety to avoid death en masse."

"How is that possible?" wondered Chamkuan who didn't get his father's point when he said cows should be put in boxes.

"Just agree or disagree, my dear," Kulang replied and was not ready to explain more on his plan as he didn't want to disclose it. "I am a married old man because I married your mother long time ago for that matter, I have no problem. It is only you who is waiting for marriage."

Chamkuan was not convinced by his father, who did not even want to convince him either. "I disagree," declared Chamkuan.

"Good for you." replied Kulang opportunely. "Now let us divide our cattle into two groups as you will have some and I shall remain with mine and do whatever I want with my cattle—including selling them." He said the last three words '…including selling them' silently so that Chamkuan could not hear.

"…but you said they should be put in boxes." said Chamkuan who had understood his father's message in low voice. "Why would you sell away cattle?"

"One doesn't tell his plan to a rebel." Kulang said. "You have rebelled against my suggestion. Why should I tell you a plan again? Let us just divide our cattle and see who will beg who between Nyadoak's son and Nyachom's son."

After the father and son divided their cattle equally, Kulang left with his cattle toward the town, leaving Chamkuan at home with his cattle. When he arrived in the town, he sold all his cattle and exchanged them with money. He pocketed his money and came back home. When he reached home he put the money in boxes waiting for the end of the flood.

Now the flood went on for several months until most of the villages' cattle died, including Chamkuan's cattle. Shortly at the end of the flood, Kulang opened his boxes, went back to the town and bought more cattle. Chamkuan regretted refusing his father's advice after he was denied milk several times by Kulang.

"*Ngoth Ka-baaw, Gat-chiek,*" he insulted when he decided to give him at last. "Didn't I tell you that we should put our cows in boxes? Opposing elders is always a suicide."

"…but you didn't tell me in detail." Chamkuan said.

"Why would people with different mothers tell secrets down to the last naked detail?" Kulang replied.

Finally, Kulang was moved to pity his son who lost his entire cattle. He gave him some cows and warned him to always learn to know of problems ahead in life. Kulang was now one of the Nuer people who were fortunate enough to escape the worst consequences of the floods because he had bought a new herd of cattle with the money he had stored. Chamkuan and the villagers followed Kulang's example in the following years.

TWENTY-SIX

The Buttock Target

South Sudan had been experiencing a constant flooding in the 1960s. There was another flood that the local people often referred to as the 'Reddish Water Flood of 1966' after a heavy rainfall.

At that time, the youth often went fishing and climbed on trees with their harpoons. The water was very clear so that the boys could see the fish moving while they were in the tree, which usually allowed them to easily throw their harpoons on their targets. This type of fishing went on for some time and the villagers were happy as more fish were brought home by their kids.

One windy day Kulang's younger son called Duer and his walking mate, Thot Jok Ruai, went fishing. Thot's father Jok Ruai Yuot was once chased by Kulang when he asked Kulang questions on the slaughtered cow. When the two peers, Duer and Thot, reached the shore, they climbed a tree as usual so that they could monitor the movement of the fish in the clear water.

Fortunately, Duer saw a fish while leaning on the tree's branch with his bunch of harpoons. "There, must be Lek (catfish)." he said.

"Oh! Lucky you," replied Thot. "Let me see if you will miss what you see."

"Over my dead body," replied Duer. "It cannot happen because a true man doesn't miss what he sees with his eyes."

Duer skillfully and speedily threw his harpoon and hit the fish. When he as well as Thot knew that the harpoon was on target, he hurriedly came down toward his harpoon because if he took much longer the fish might escape the harpoon and run.

The other harpoons Duer had left up on the tree as their attention was on the target. When he bent down trying to bring

So you have brought the fish home with your buttock, my son!

out the fish from the harpoon inside the water, one of his harpoons that he had left on the tree fell and hit him on the buttock.

Alas, the boy could not feel the pain as his attention was on the very big fish he had caught. Duer, instead of removing the harpoon from his buttock, ran happily home with blood flowing from the fish as well as himself. He was running to his father, Kulang. Perhaps he wanted to be glorified and praised for managing to get a fish as big as he had caught.

When Kulang saw him come with speed, he got surprised and asked his son of why he was running. The boy replied that he had harpooned a fish.

"*Kachilooj!*" yelled Kulang with cheerfulness in his face. "So you have brought the fish home with your buttock, my son! How strong is this Pilual generation? How will animals' Pilual generation be if human's Pilual generation could be as strong as such?"

"You are my true son, Thontuot." he continued. "You are not Nyachom's son. Chamkuan is the Nyachom's son." From that very day Kulang was impressed by his younger son, Duer, who did great by bringing 'Lek' home with his buttock unlike his older son, Chamkuan, who only gave him stress.

TWENTY-SEVEN

Kulang's Small-scale Farming

Agriculture and livestock are the main sources of livelihood across the Nuer land especially in the rural areas. Cultivation always depends on rainfall as most farmers depend on rain fed farming.

In the year 1950, Kulang made a vast field for a small scale-farm in Toch. His small-scale farm had eight unit areas called feddans. Kulang, under all odds, was a smallholder farmer who produced much of the food that landed on his kids' plates as well as himself. He knew very well how to identify early warnings of impeding weather threats, water harvesting and mixed farming methods that allowed him to blend fast-maturing and drought-resistant crops.

In that particular farming season, Kulang, divided the eight feddans into two. Four units on the plain land which was arable for crops to grow well in case the dry season commenced. The other four units were on the plateau land which was high ground for crops to grow well in case of heavy seasonal rainfall.

The anthropologists called Kulang's type of agriculture 'horticulture' rather than farming because it was done like simple gardening and was supplementary to hunting and gathering. It differs from farming also in its technology. Cereals, primarily sorghum and maize, millet and rice are the leading staple crops in the Nuer land and even across South Sudan.

One year later, there was too much rain in the whole land. Due to that excessive rainfall, most of the village's crops were destroyed, including Kulang's crops on the plain land, leaving him only with the other farm in the highlands. A short time after the harvest, the villagers began to talk and complain about the hunger and famine that badly hit their village.

"Kuoth-nhial (God of heaven) has punished us this year." said one of the farmers.

"Indeed, Deng-Taath must be angry of us." replied another farmer.

"Yes He must be." confirmed the third one.

"Is there a famine in this land, brothers?" Kulang asked them arrogantly. The lazy farmers listened with their mouth wide open as it was unbelievable for one of their men to doubt the presence of the famine. They were unable to imagine how Kulang was living his life comfortably in the famine-hit land. One of them who was kind enough managed to answer him. "Yes there is a famine." he was told.

"WO!" yelled Kulang angrily upon hearing the confirmation of the existence of the famine in the land. "It is not fair for you guys to blame the good God for your hunger and famine and not your laziness. Didn't you know that the rain has no enemy because it falls everywhere in the land? Why was I not punished by Deng-Taath? Am I not his descendent? Is it not your refusal of work? Will this hunger reach my home? People are expert only in putting their hands in their laps, and like drinking wine in the morning at different homes expecting God to bring them food. People do not know that even God does not directly give His pastors and servants free food. God gave them eyes and hands to help themselves. If you guys don't work hard, you will end up visiting other people's homes every time and they will never visit you. It is better to be visited or exchange visit than visiting people every now and then like the visitors of my home."

A story is told about laziness. The rain god had been smiling for the whole night. The roads were muddy and the potholes were filled to the brim. It was the day for the market and the farmer was riding the cart along the country road. He had to reach the market early so that he could sell his hay. It was very difficult for the horses to drag the load through the deep mud.

On his journey, suddenly the wheels of the horse cart sank into the mire. The more the horse pulled, the deeper the wheel sank. The farmer climbed down from his seat and stood beside his cart. He searched all around but could not find anyone around to help him.

Cursing his bad luck, he looked dejected and defeated. He didn't make the slightest effort to get down on the wheel and lift it up by himself. Instead he started cursing his luck for what happened.

Looking up at the sky, he started shouting at God, "I am so unlucky! Why has this happened to me? Oh God, come down to help me."

After a long wait, God finally appeared before him.

He asked the farmer, "Do you think you can move the chariot by simply looking at it and whining about it? Nobody will help you unless you make some effort to help yourself. Did you try to get the wheel out of the pothole by yourself? Get up and put your shoulder to wheel and you will soon find the way out."

The farmer was ashamed of himself. He bent down and put his shoulder to the wheel and urged on the horses. In no time, the wheel was out of the mire. The farmer learnt his lesson. He thanked God and carried on his journey happily.

Kulang talked to the farmers and said, "Almighty Kuoth-Nhial helps only those who help themselves." The village farmers were encouraged by Kulang's speech against laziness and they promised to harvest more cereals in the next planting season.

The farmers finally decided to go to their homes speechless as most of them were touched by Kulang's facts about farming and life.

"Let me tell you," Kulang told them when he saw them go. "In future, make your farming in an area that consists of both plain and plateau lands for the safety of one side during worse time of relief, frontal or convectional rainfalls or even in an excessive flood or drought as nobody knows about tomorrow and next tomorrow."

TWENTY-EIGHT

The Young Men Regret

One day around morning time, Kulang took his cattle to the bush for grazing. While he was away, five young men arrived and sat at the side of his Luak. Nyachom served them with water when she saw them. After the young men had drunk water, they began to enjoy their snuff with their noises so that they could continuously sneeze and enjoy. The young men were enjoying while resting with their back on the Luak's wall when Kulang arrived.

Kulang knew that people had arrived in his absence so he played a trick against them. He entered the Luak tiptoeing and creeping without even breathing like someone hunting animals or birds. He quietly and speedily pulled a long stick and started to hit the youth with his eyes closed as if he did not know they were people.

When it came to acting, Kulang was the number one in the land. He could even pretend to be dead and people would cry when in fact he was alive. Now he had to get rid of the poor young men who were enjoying themselves inside the Lua*k*.

"What is that hissing in my Luak?" he cried while hitting the young people pretending to have heard a sound of a cobra-snake.

"*Gat-Toat! Gat-Toat!*" cried the young men. "We are people who have just arrived."

"Wa, White fabrication!" he said while continuing hitting. "People don't hiss like snakes. You are liars, aren't you? So don't falsely pretend to be young people when it's beyond doubts that you are snakes. I had never hissed when I was young and I don't hiss now. Does it mean I am not human? You are snakes not young men, my kids."

After he satisfied himself by beating the poor youth several times, he finally came to his consciousness since he knew the boys had paid the price of any accommodation that they might have received from Nyachom with the beating that he had done.

"So," he continued. "The youth of nowadays make sounds like snakes and enjoy snuff with their noses so that they sneeze?"

The angry youth went silent because they were badly hurt by Kulang who pretended to be unaware of their existence. The poor youth sorrowfully left and never attempted to visit Kulang ever again in their lifetime. Kulang became happy with his wonderful trick in hurting and chasing the young men who had nearly eaten with him.

Shortly after he got rid of the youth, another man who was leading a goat arrived at his home. The man had come from afar and was very thirsty after a long journey in a hot day. Whenever he moved further he would see a freshwater stream ahead of him but when he went near, the freshwater stream disappeared, only to appear again a little further on until he decided to take rest at a nearby home which was Kulang's home. The Nuer call that fooling freshwater as 'thirst'.

"Hi, cousin," Kulang called from afar when he saw the man was coming leading his goat. "Is that your dog?"

"No brother haha!" The man answered cheerfully with laughter thinking that the owner of the home was welcoming him. "It is not a dog but a goat."

"I am not talking to you. I am talking to the goat." he answered sharply, and the man was saddened by that.

"Do you think I am a dog?" the man asked angrily.

"I do not know brother." Kulang said. "May be but I am not sure. Do you come to tell me that you are a dog in my home? I do not want to hear more of you being a dog or goat. The road has not ended here, Gar-guur."

The man became very sad and shifted from resting at Kulang's home and instead went to a different home. Kulang became happy after he got rid of the man who had almost rested at his home.

TWENTY-NINE

Kulang Interrupts the Soldiers

The former Anyanya movement used guerrilla warfare against the Sudanese government in Khartoum. They voluntarily mobilized themselves into small group of combatants including: paramilitary recruits, armed civilians, or irregulars; and used military tactics including ambushes, interruption, raids, petty warfare, hit and run tactics, and mobility, to fight a larger or smaller Sudanese armed force.

Most of the Anyanya had no guns but used spears, machetes, and other sharp instruments that could hurt an enemy. During any battle time, as many as fifty trained and untrained men would be speedily marching forward to the enemy, their guns waiting for their owners to be killed as the rest continue the fight. They used to get their guns and ammunitions from the government troops. Their revolutionary songs boosted their morale in fighting the war empty handed.

One winter day as the Anyanya soldiers were preparing to launch an attack against the government's barracks, Kulang arrived at their military garrison with food in his hand. He intended to interrupt them as he was fed up with their continuous looting in the villages.

When he arrived, he asked the group of the soldiers who were busy making their morning parade drilling and marching to exhibit their military strength in their forthcoming battle in one of the nearby government barracks in Fangak.

"My sons," he began in a fatherly voice. "My food is tasteless. May you give it salt?"

Do you think they are idiots, looters and thieves like you?

"Gat-Toat, we do not have salt." one of the soldiers replied while busy.

"Alas!" wondered Kulang. "This revolution of yours kills cattle without salt! What kind of fake revolution is this without salt!"

The soldiers were angered by Kulang's statements and they decided that he would never be given meat if any cow was to be slaughtered. Kulang went and sat under a big tree, not far from where soldiers were parading.

As he was sitting under the shade of a tree, a dog came passing him by. On seeing the dog, he threw his heavy fighting stick at the dog.

"Stupid dog," he insulted with loud voice that was heard from afar by the soldiers. "Why are you looking at our brave human-soldiers? Are they your brothers? Do you think they are idiots, looters and thieves like you? When will your dog-soldiers join bushes against the Arab-dogs in Khartoum? Do you think these soldiers are sons of women who fight with their eyes shut during battles?"

The soldiers knew at last that Kulang was actually not insulting the dog but was insulting them. Finally, he left for his house after a successful mission.

THIRTY

The Fight over Salt

While Kulang and his wife Nyachom were in a fishing camp at the riverbank doing their yearly fishing, there was a company of soldiers moving around that area, looking for people to get fish from. They saw Kulang and his wife and went directly to ask them for fish.

While there, they saw a bottle of salt and decided to take it forcefully, as it was the culture of the rebel-army to forcefully take things from civilians. The soldiers started to fight over who should take the bottle of salt.

'Fighting' according to the Nuer Tales, was believed to be grown among people by fox when he provoked the two friendly workers to fight. One of the two men was a fisherman and the other was a hunter. If one was good in fishing, the other one was competent in hunting. The two had been good friends until the fox decided to separate them in a ceaseless fight.

The fox went to the river and checked the net of the fisherman which had caught a catfish. The fox took the catfish from the fisherman's net and put it in the hunter's net which had seized a bird in the nearby bush. The fox again took the bird which was caught by the hunter's net and put it in the river in the fisherman's net.

In the morning, each went to check his net but unfortunately, they found what the fox did. Each ran home angrily accusing each other of having stolen each other's food. Today, people around the world keep fighting each other individually or in groups.

The rebels were fighting over the bottle of salt when Kulang saw them and asked them to stop fighting over the salt. He asked the rebel-soldiers: "Didn't you recognize it?"

The soldiers replied that they had recognized it and that it was salt.

At that point Kulang said: "Well, if it is salt, will you eat it? Won't you die because it belongs to your Arab-enemy? Could it be that because you are kids that you don't know that anything that comes from an enemy kills? Uniform doesn't share anything enemy-made except for guns." Kulang actually was an intelligent philosopher with a sweet tongue which convinced people speedily.

On hearing that, the soldiers stopped and left the salt because they were convinced by Kulang with a fabricated omen.

It has been said that when brothers fight, a stranger always benefits. There was a certain traveler on one hot summer day. He hired a donkey and set out on a journey. The owner of the donkey was following behind to drive the animal.

At mid-day, they decided to rest for some time but couldn't find any shady place around. So, the traveler decided to rest in the shade of the donkey. But the owner didn't let him do so as he himself wanted to sit in its shadow. "How can you refuse me the shadow of a donkey that I have hired with the money I paid you?" asked the traveler furiously.

"But you have paid for the ride, not for resting in its shadow." retorted the owner. The argument went on between the two. When the donkey saw that the owner and the hirer were busy fighting, he took to his heels and was soon out of the two's sights.

None of the soldiers who were fighting over Kulang's salt claimed it and Kulang succeeded in protecting his salt by making up things in order to scare them.

THIRTY-ONE

Nyachom's Mother Regrets

A mother and father in-law do not eat or drink at their daughter's home unless a goat or cow is slaughtered for them to be officially welcomed as custom demands. They are only allowed when their daughter's children get married.

One day, Nyachom's mother visited her. It was at noon time when she arrived. Nyachom made a very nice butter mixed food for her mother. After resting for a while, the mother left for her home at Tharkotda-Ler. Kulang was going to chase her away had she not gone quickly.

At the end of fourteen days, she returned back again. Nyachom happily welcomed her again with nice food. In the evening hours, the mother in-law informed Kulang so she could officially go. However, he instead acted as if he were deaf and dumb because he was fed up of her visits.

"I have to go back now, son." said the mother in-law, looking down in respect to her in-law. But Kulang could not say a word.

"My dear son," she said again thinking that her son in-law had not listened to her at first. "I need to go back to Tharkotda-Ler." There was silence again. She tried and tried but Kulang would not reply.

When Nyachom's mother detected that Kulang didn't want to talk to her, she turned away to her daughter's hut to inform her for her to go. Now the mother in-law was endorsed by her daughter Nyachom and she decided to finally go to her home.

The only lane that could lead her out of her daughter's home passed near Kulang's Luak. When she arrived near the entrance of the Luak so as to leave, Kulang brought out his head, leaving other parts of his body inside the *Luak*, and called so that his voice could be heard by his mother in-law.

"Nyachom! Nyachom!" he angrily called, and Nyachom suddenly responded with the sharp African women's voice.

"Weeew!" she cried and ran toward her husband only to get disappointed.

"What kind of day-walking does your mother have?" Kulang said when Nyachom reached, still with a loud voice so that his mother in-law could not miss it. "Let her not come at day time again or else she will die on the way between two homes. Give her that important thing that she doesn't have at her home. A day-visitor is only given cooked millet." Kulang made a warning that his mother-in-law took with full consideration and she never came back again as she was ashamed and disappointed by her son in-law.

The Nuer people treat marriage, the foundation of any given society, as a union for life between a man and a woman. The extended family members either on the man's side or the woman's side are always connected by the marriage. They stay friendly praising their good deeds and compromising their bad deeds. Sometimes, the two families exert a very strong influence on marriage and this influence has on many occasions had a bad effect on the marriages, resulting in either regret, unhappiness, or even a total disintegration of the marriage.

According to the Nuer culture, the wife is married with contribution from the entire wide lineage of those who meet at the fourth or fifth great grandfather. The same thing also happens when a daughter is married. The wife is expected to call every other member of the family Guan-gan or 'Kids' father' that means she is to marry not only her husband (except in sexual matters) but the whole family and the clan that shares the same names and so forth.

Sometimes a wife easily falls out with her mother in-law (her husband's mother) but it is very rare for a husband to have grudges with his mother in-law. Kulang had now broken the respect by the offensive in parable against his mother in-law who, in Nuer culture, is not even watched for so long but given a little glance in respect, leave alone raising your voice against her.

THIRTY-TWO

Kulang Insults his Bride

The love of cattle by the Nuer can be dated back to the ancient time. The Nuer people always care for their beloved animals, sleeping next to them at night, grazing them by day. Cow fresh dung or manure is not thrown away according to the Nuer culture. It is instead scattered and exposed to the sun to dry. In the evening they are collected and put together and set fire in them so that its smoke drives away mosquitoes and other insects that disturb the cattle.

Kulang sat around his burning campfire and picked up the cooled ash called '*puok*' on the edge of the fire and rubbed it on his favourite oxen's back to clean it. When he finished cleaning his oxen, he sat down again and now the fire was very wild.

He put a cucumber in the fire and eagerly waited for it to roast. He didn't want any soul to pass by or talk to him while he was expecting his cucumber to roast well before the evening dinner. He slapped many calves many times that tried to sleep near the burning fire because of his cucumber's safety.

Shortly, his beautiful bride whose cooking ritual was finalized the day before came in order to take some fire to let her cook in the women's hut. Now Kulang was angered by the move because his cucumber was roasting inside the fire-bank and he didn't want to be disturbed.

Because the woman was new, Kulang didn't want to directly warn her on taking any fire-log while his cucumber was inside the fire. He started to beat his Thom when he noticed that the bride was near to the fireplace and wanted to take the fire. He didn't want the wife to notice and see his cucumber at all cost.

"*Ekuledien igatot igatot!*" he began with his Thom. Nyachom jumped to her feet and left what she was doing to listen to Kulang's message through Thom to avoid troublesomeness because she knew all Kulang's parables.

"*Kuenyenitony-mach eho cha-degai. Chia kulang pal, chia wa ka tongboor-kooy,*" he continued beating "*inyachom ha luek nyakdu han Gat-Toat cha gaal ke liel kath.*"

The conclusion of the Thom's sound was vile and disgusting to his new bride and in general about women as Nuer men usually respect women when it came to insulting. There are some insults which Nuer men never use against women not even in a fight, be it family wives or wives of other people no matter what they did to men. Kulang had to use any tactic for the safety of his cucumber despite the dignity of the bride.

Right from there Nyachom understood that Kulang didn't want the bride to take any fire log. She speedily ran to the bride and stopped her from taking the fire and instead directed her to bring the fire from the neighbour's home. Nyachom didn't tell her co-wife the insult meanwhile, Kulang's cucumber was safe and peace returned again in the family.

THIRTY-THREE

Kulang in the Church

It was Christmas Day when Moses Chuol Juach, the Executive Director of Fangak, invited Kulang to attend the Christmas prayers with him in the church. The Executive Director was a kind man who was fond of walking with many people irrespective of their wealth status or ages. Perhaps it might be his strong belief in trying to convert the natives to Christianity.

The two spent the night together at the Executive Director's home waiting for the morning for them to hear the word of God after the birth of the baby Jesus Christ.

In the morning time, the two entered the church and the prayers began.

"In the name of the Father, and of the Son, and of the Holy Spirit, Amen." The Pastor began the Trinitarian formula with all the congregation standing except Kulang.

"Holy Father and maker of heaven and earth," the pastor continued the opening prayer. "You have made all things according to your word. God of flesh, you have made us the head of creation. We are here to worship you and praise your name. May our worship be accepted by you? Let us ride on the wings of our praises and refresh our spirits in you. As we begin today, guide us toward your will…Amen."

It was the first time Kulang had attended church prayers in his entire life since most of the villagers had converted to Christianity. The prayers went on for a quite long time but Kulang was not always interested in a place where people could not eat or drink anything. Now the church choir started to sing loudly and the church was as noisy as a heavy thunderstorm. After the choirs had finished their emotional song, the pastor stepped forward happily to read a verse from the Holy Bible.

"Brothers and Sisters, Sons and Daughters, Fathers and Mothers, Good morning," said the pastor with a loud voice. "Today we have received the lord. If you have a Bible kindly open Matthew 1:2. But, if you do not have, then follow me,"

"…And she shall bring forth a son," the pastor began reading from the bible. "And thou shall call his name Jesus: for he shall save his people from their sins."

Kulang surprisingly looked at all the ladies including the female choir members as if to see exactly the one who had been said to bring forth a son.

"Will the woman in the bible give birth to a son now?" he asked the pastor with his hand raised up expecting to be given an answer.

"No!" the Executive Director simply approached him with a smile on his face and put down Kulang's hand. "People do not ask questions when the pastor is reading a Bible. That woman is not here. It is Mary the virgin mother of Jesus Christ, son of God the saviour."

"Jesus Christ who?" he demanded. "Where is that virgin? How would a little child save the world? I think we are not included because a child cannot save old people. We should go then." He stood up and decided to go but he was forced to sit down by the Executive Director.

When he sat he continued talking "Aha! If your Virgin Mary had been beaten by someone like me, believe me, Gatgualen, she would have taken people to the place of the child's father." Kulang said beaming.

The Executive Director tried different ways to convince him but to no avail.

At that point, the prayers were declared over by the pastor and everyone was told to shake hands with their neighbours. The Executive Director tried to greet Kulang but he resisted at first by saying: "Haven't we come together?" The Executive Director insisted until he gave him his hand but refused to greet his neighbours.

The choirs and all the congregation were morally singing the Christ's night birth song:

"*Oh Holy Night! The stars are brightly shining.*"

Kulang rebuked a young man by his side when he was loudly singing and he felt disturbed.

"Hi you! Gat-Chiek, what kind of night and shining stars do you talk about?" he furiously asked. "Don't you know its day time now?" He was ignored as the people were very happy for the birth of the Christ. The song went on and on:

It is the night of the dear Saviour's birth.
Long lay the world in sin and error pining.
Till He appeared and the Spirit felt its worth.

A thrill of hope the weary world rejoices,
For yonder breaks a new and glorious morn.
Fall on your knees! Oh, hear the angel voices!
O night divine, the night when Christ was born.

Now the pastor had to take Kulang by hand to his house. When the two men arrived home they were served with big mango juice cups by the pastor's wife. Kulang drank the first cup at once. He took the other and restored his consciousness as if to take rest after a long stress in the church. If one didn't see Kulang drinking his cups of juice, he would think that he might have poured them down.

"*Gatgualen,*" he said. "To be sincere with you, all the speeches and verses in the Church were not interesting to me. They instead made me hate the life of this world. The yellow cups that I have just drunk have with no doubts interested me more than the Church's Bible."

The pastor smiled and opened his Bible to read a verse for Kulang. "My brother, Our Lord Jesus told His disciples this message; 'Therefore I tell you, do not worry about your life, what you will eat, or about your body, what you will wear.' So believe only in the Holy Trinity." The pastor closed his Bible.

Kulang didn't understand the meaning of the verse that was just read at home by the pastor. He instead asked more questions. "Which Jesus? Do you mean the unborn child?" he asked surprisingly.

The pastor told him that the juice would be available anytime if he could go to church always.

"If this juice is available in the church, believe me I will always be the first person to read the Bible and even sing alone." he said and there was laughter in the hut.

THIRTY-FOUR

Kulang Insults the Head Chief

Elections were held for candidates contesting for the post of Head Chief in the land of Paguir in Fangak area. The elections results were announced and a man by the name Nyang Kiy Wuor, won with a huge number of votes. The name 'Nyang' in Nuer literally means 'crocodile'. So he was declared the official head chief to deal with the affairs of the local people.

Nyang Kiy Wuor had just come from town where he had studied and even worked in the police unit. He was an educated man who did his studies in the northern towns. News of Nyang's success in the elections reached many villages far away including the village of Toch, where Kulang lived.

When Kulang heard that Nyang had won, he said bad words against the elected Head Chief. "You, Chiengkuaj-boor!" he called. "You have brought from the river a wild crocodile and elect him? Who will you blame when he starts to eat you? You cannot expect a crocodile to stay with people without eating them. Is it not the same crocodile that was even recognized by his father, Kiy, who tossed him away by taking him to town in pretext of studying? You have made a grave mistake by appointing him."

Kulang disliked head chiefs and gave them many bad names

because he was let down by them when a man he once healed won a court case against him.

In the past Kulang had treated a man whose rib was broken and he had to cut a tiny stick from the tree and put it in the place of the broken rib as traditional doctors do. The man who was cured by Kulang became happy and gave him a heifer. After sometime the heifer produced three other calves.

When the man who gave the cow to Kulang, knew that his heifer that he had given to Kulang, had produced more calves, he went to the court and claimed all of them back. Kulang tried many means in defense but were to no avail. And that was the genesis of Kulang hating the head chiefs including the newly elected head chief.

"Government officials are wise sons and daughters of women who gather themselves to loot the poor people." he angrily said to the people in his village right after he lost the court case. "I will never trust anybody working for the government in my life."

The dispute of Kulang and the other person whom he had treated had occurred sometime back, but Kulang had now lost confidence in all the Court levels. As a result, he mistrusted the whole local judicial system and this was the reason for him to dislike the new Chief. He had completely lost hope in the government and its agents.

At that point, news of Nyang Kiy Wuor's fair justice reached everywhere in the land. Everyone was praising Chief Nyang for his fair judgment and talent in judging unlike other judges.

Kulang now became happy but was afraid of the insults he had made when Nyang was elected. Everyone including the chief Nyang himself had heard of Kulang's insults when he termed him to be a 'crocodile'. But Kulang knew what to say to convince the chief as he was perfect when it came to how to convince people. His tongue was very sweet and bad sometimes.

When he arrived at Paguir, where the chief was working, he approached him with smile and gratitude: "*Donyang! Donyang!*" he called while grabbing the chief to congratulate him on winning the elections. The chief was glad at being congratulated and called '*Donyang*' or a child of a crocodile and not the crocodile as Kulang had said before.

"I have a case, Kuar Donyang." Kulang finally said, after he was welcomed and served with water. He narrated his entire story until the chief decided to call the man who was sued in court by him. The man arrived at last.

"Kuar Chief," Kulang began. "To make the long story short, what I really need now is the stick I had put in the place of this man's rib when I treated him before." he said that while removing his sharp knife from his goat-skin bag as if to cut the man's stomach.

The defendant shivered and his eyes turned to red like an old bull being slaughtered. His face changed with fright and fear when he saw Kulang bring out his sharp knife before the court.

"Yes, you are right, Kulang." said Nyang the chief, and pointing at his bodyguards as to help in cutting the man's stomach. "Take the man outside, soldiers, for Kulang to remove his stick and let the man take his four cows."

The man shook again more and promised to bring back the

cows. Kulang became happy and respected Nyang Kiy Wuor for his fair judgment. The man became regretful for his actions.

This was like a certain girl who, despite her beauty, was unhappy and promised to marry only a man who would make her laugh or smile. Many young men in the village and beyond tried in vain to make her laugh or at least smile but she could not. One day, a young man promised to make her laugh louder but people could not believe him.

The boy collected a straw ring used by women in carrying heavy loads on their heads. The boy left toward the place that the beautiful girl used to sit. When he arrived, he went straight to the biggest tree and put the straw ring against the trunk and held it with his head.

"Come on please," he called the girl. "Help me lift this tree on my head. I want to carry it home."

Upon hearing that, the beautiful girl fell down in ceaselessly laughter that surprised many.

"You are a congenital liar, aren't you?" she said with mirth, all her well-placed white teeth out. "How on the earth can a tree be carried?"

Finally, the clever boy took home the beautiful girl instead of the tree. Because he made her laugh louder than was expected.

THIRTY-FIVE

Kulang and Tut Kuach Diew

The 1960s flood that covered Sudan displaced many people in the land of Fangak and its surroundings. Little was done by building dykes and bridges for the flood to at least reduce the flow of water. There was a bridge, which was built at the border of Thiang-Nuer and Lak-Nuer, in order to prevent the water from destroying homes, farms and gardens. Each side of the bridge fell to each of the two sisterly communities, Thiang and Lak. The water from the flood was flowing from the side of Thiang to the side of Lak, because the river was high on one side. It was believed that most of the fish could go with the flowing of the water. That progress angered Kulang, who took his Kueny-goor (stool) toward the house of his clan-mate, Tut Kuach Diew.

Kulang, upon arrival, was served with water and smoking pipe by his clan-mate but still he was not happy.

"My friend," he began. "I have not come on a friendly visit as usual. But I want to know how many days has it been with this disturbing flood that wants to take away our life."

"Seven days now." Tut simply replied.

"But do you see the bad part of this flood, cousin?" Kulang asked, glaring at Tut.

The Nuer elders say, 'Every frog croaks in its place in the lake.' That saying means people may suffer the same problem but they may not know that they are suffering together until the meeting day arrives. Now Kulang thought he was the only person being disturbed by heavy flood until he found his clan-mate was disturbed too.

"Yes, I do very well as you do." Tut retorted, while smoking his long pipe. "This flood came with more fish but the bad part is that useless bridge between us and the Lak community. It is very sad seeing our fish going to the side of Lak every now and then."

"That is the saddest part of it, cousin." Kulang said sadly while stretching his hand to collect the long pipe from him. "Honestly, I have come to discuss this issue with you as there are no elders in our community apart from two of us. The God of our ancestors must have sided with Lak-Nuer by sending away our fish to their land."

"Yes, definitely true." confirmed Tut, and started to change his sitting style. "Our cousins, Lak, have their own Choulwich called Kuok-Lak. He must be the one transferring our fish to them."

"Very sad," Kulang said, putting down the pipe. "I could not believe my eyes when I saw Tilapia, catfish, Tiger fish, Nile perch, Barbell, and many more big fat fish jumping speedily to the Lak side from our side. Now we have known the cause of our fish's migration to Lak side. What is the way forward to deal with Choulwich-Lak, cousin?"

"The solution is very easy, cousin." said Tut. "One of us must die and fight the Lak's god bravely to return the flow of water to our side for the safety of our upcoming generations otherwise they will be poor as all fish will always go to Lak side."

"Die?" asked Kulang surprised.

"Die." confirmed Tut.

"That is exactly the solution. Thank you for speaking out what is in my mind." said Kulang happily. "Then I have to die so that I get rid of Kuok-Lak in battle."

"It is not fair." Tut replied. "I am the one to die because I have no forgiveness when it comes to fight. I must deal away strongly with Kuok-Lak. I must be Kuok-Thiang and I will never let you down, I swear."

The two old men began to debate on who to die since each of them was angered by the continuous flow of water to Lak's side. The debate went on for a long time. Each was giving the advantages of his death towards the solution.

It got to the point where the two took all their nets to the river and scattered them in the river such that only water could pass and fish would return once passed through the nets. The two old men made that trick for some days until they knew the trick could not control the movement of the fish.

After two months in heavy rain supported by an angry thunderstorm, Tut died as per the curse and promise he had made. His body was not found as it went away with the thunderstorm. Now Tut was going to be the Chuol-wich as per the custom. Kulang took two of his oxen and slaughtered them in the holy shrine so that he could talk to the deceased.

Suddenly the clouds started gathering early in the morning and all the villagers were longing to see their Chuol-wich who had died sometimes back. Women sat on mats on the ground and

Now we have known the cause of our fishes' migration to Lak side.

old men sat on their stools brought by their children who chose to stand.

"Oh God of our ancestors, give us a word with your servant that you took from us." said one of the old men

"*Gatgualen! Gatdila! Chuol-wichda!*" Kulang began angrily as custom demands "Come to us if you meant the words that you said last time." After a short while the man was seen up in the sky supported by the heavy clouds and he was smiling. Tut was seen in the clouds with the same clothes that he was wearing when he died in a thunderstorm.

"You said it clear last time," continued Kulang. "That you would be the one to die but I have no doubt now on your bravery. Now start to shift the flow of the water tonight if you are a true god. And bring prosperity to all including our Lak brothers."

The man was gone after Kulang had finished talking to him and there were no more wonders in the land of Thiang and Lak for a long period of time. Perhaps, Tut defeated Kuok-Lak in a fight for uniting the two sisterly communities.

THIRTY-SIX

Kulang at the Marriage Ceremony

The marriage celebration according to the Nuer people is done after the haggling and bargaining of the cows is made. On the fixed day all the man's family and his friends go to the home of the girl's kin in a festival mood, leading the needed cows. Once they arrived, they would find the girl's kin people ready waiting for them. After greeting each other by clan or nick names, the young people and women would start the celebration by dancing, wailing and singing the traditional songs until dusk falls.

Then, they would eat and drink in groups. Meanwhile the old men would drink white wine and chat with their peers or age mates from each side. They would talk of the olden days in comparison to the current time, evaluating the life of the great grandfathers, their time and the future generations. Dancing and eating together shows the blessing of the marriage and it is the legalization of its contract.

Kulang, in his whole life, verbally spoke little to his wife Nyachom but instead talked more in nonverbal cues when visitors or soldiers came home to keep his secrets safe as he was a man who kept to himself and his wife alone. His facial expressions, gestures, posture, tone of voice, and the level of eye contact were his powerful communications which were known by none in the land other than

Nyachom. His relatives and children could not understand his nonverbal forms but Nyachom knew it as well as Kulang knew it. Nyachom took good care of Kulang's words not in what he said but how he said them.

One day Kulang went to a marriage ceremony in a neighbouring village. Nyachom was away cutting grass and sisal leaves to make fans for her husband and kids when her husband left for the marriage ceremony without informing her.

When she arrived home, she found her husband was not there. Nyachom became confused of what to do because her husband left without deciding which dish would be cooked by her. She finally decided to go in order to ask him about the type of the food to be cooked. But how was she going to ask him at an important occasion like marriage?

The marriage ceremony was full of people from different backgrounds in the land and it was difficult for a woman to call a man during such an occasion.

Nyachom obviously knew what she would do. She put on her best traditional clothes for weddings including her 'Noh' or hair and her Tang-Yoka (a ponytail cut from a cow's tail and tied at the head of a stick).

When she arrived at the venue, she began to sing her traditional song as everyone had their songs. All the participants' attention were drawn by her beautiful voice and dance. Everyone wanted to go and dance with her but Kulang told them that it was his wife, and he would dance with her because he guessed that Nyachom had come with an urgent message.

When she arrived at the playground, she began to sing her traditional song as everyone had their songs.

"I am in trouble." she said in a song. "Shall I make *Kop* or *Piech*?"

All people were enjoying the song with their mouths open and didn't know that Nyachom was coming to send a message to her husband. Kulang who clearly understood the message prepared himself by clearing his throat to sing back in response to Nyachom's traditional song and dance.

"*Thak-jioh Nyimar Mi Ci Loj Tol e-hook*," he lamented as he was marching towards Nyachom to sing his song. "Nyachom, let it be *Kop* and give it *Lieth-yang*. If you make it *Piech* it is your choice but put the *Lieth-yang* to its tail."

Then Nyachom returned after she fully got the message that she had been needing from her husband. The crowd and Kulang went back to the occasion. They did not know exactly that Kulang and his wife had exchanged words through the songs.

THIRTY-SEVEN

Kulang and the Deaf Man

One day Kulang went to the home of a man who had lost his hearing due to an unknown occurrence many years ago. He had been deaf for a long time and at first he used to talk to his wives and children normally due to the fact that he only lost sense of hearing. But when the unknown infection went on he began to talk to them through the help of sign language.

When the man went deaf, most of the villagers constantly flooded him with apologies and grief. He was surrounded with pity since he was a good man in the village. The people always told him that going deaf was not the end of the world. They had always reminded him to keep healthy thoughts in his mind because his life would move on until God finalized his natural end.

When Kulang arrived, he first went to the man's place as per the Nuer custom. "*Maale?*" he greeted but no one answered. "*Maale Jo!*" he repeated but the deaf man could not answer him back as he did not hear Kulang and he was busy knitting robes for his cows.

Kulang turned to the women and asked them why the man could not answer him.

"What is the name of this man that I have been calling for years and doesn't want to answer back my greetings?" he asked furiously.

"Something happened to him some couple of years ago. He has a hearing problem that was the reason why he failed to answer back your greetings." he was told.

"Was it a result of sickness when it happened." he asked wretchedly.

Ah, where is his problem here if he eats?

"No!" he was told. "He had not fallen sick."

"Well, does he eat?" he asked.

"Of course he does!" he was told.

"Ah, where is his problem here if he eats?" he asked in derision. The women could not answer him as they felt mocked by Kulang.

"Well, there is no problem at all if he sees and eats what is given to him." Kulang continued when no one dared to talk to him. "Being deaf is not a bad thing and it is indeed not something to grieve. This man is the luckiest man in the whole world due to the fact that no one will ever disturb him.

"This world has nothing good to be heard with ears. Only good things to be eaten with mouths; I would have cried if it was his mouth that didn't eat but because it is his ears, he is more than lucky. I would be glad if I were in his place, since, I am tired of listening to baloney from lazy people of this world in the names of visitors. I will ask Kuoth-Nhial to turn my hearing aids off and enter a realm of total silence when visitors come and opens the hearing back when they go so that I listen only to my dear wife Nyachom."

Kulang hated having houseguests even if they were his immediate family members. He really valued his privacy and he never for a single night slept in someone's home. That was his nature.

THIRTY-EIGHT

Kulang Identifies his Likes

The sun was shining brightly and everyone was in their huts and then suddenly the clouds began to gather themselves from nowhere and started to pour down. That rain was believed to be raining very heavily in the land. Because it came suddenly, most of the women in the land did not have a chance to collect firewood for cooking. If it rained in the village, most of the people would sleep without food because all the firewood, the only means for cooking, would get soaked with water.

Kulang was in his *Luak* when it was bucketing down so profoundly. Now the rain pitter-pattered as it reduced while Kulang was eagerly waiting for his evening meal.

Nyachom knew all the traditional fire building methods very well. She made a fire and brought out her reserved kindling and sticks to cook for her husband who could not tolerate the coldness of the weather without food.

Nyachom suddenly appeared inside the *Luak* carrying Kulang's evening meal. She knelt down, put the food before him, greeted him with a smile and dispersed.

Kneeling down before men in the Nuer culture is a symbolic act to show men's dominion over wives and female subordination to their husbands.

Kulang served himself and pushed aside the empty dish waiting for Nyachom to take it back. He didn't always follow the culture of eating. When a man was given food, whether a big or small quantity, he would leave a little leftover in the dish to be eaten by his wife. Now Kulang left the dish the same way it was bought from the market.

"A rain like this!" he said to himself, feeling full and pretty happy. "All lazy women who call themselves men and who are being ruled by their wives in their homes will not eat tonight. But I believe, cobra-men like Dhuoh Duoh of Lak, Malual Beliu and Jut Pech, of western Nile plus Tung-kuey of Nyalual, will certainly eat tonight with me as they rule their women like me." The men might have shared similar characters or interests with him.

Whenever a dish was put before him by Nyachom, he would eat all he could, even when he knew he had had more than he wanted bodily. What always lingered in his mind after any meal was the thought of getting back the taste of it again. They say people of the same sort or with the same tastes and interests walk and understand each other. Kulang always liked to praise some of the men in different lands though they had never stayed together with him.

He knew who were the lazy men or hard working people in the lands.

A story about work is told of a lazy grasshopper. One fine sunny day in the winter season, a grasshopper was busking in the warm sun. But he was very hungry, as he had not eaten anything the previous night. The lazy grasshopper looked about to find something to soothe his hunger.

Suddenly, he saw few ants carrying grains into their hole. He went up to the ants and begged them. "Can you, please, spare few grains for me. I haven't eaten anything since yesterday. So I am almost starving to death."

One of the ants asked the grasshopper, "What were you doing the whole summer? Why didn't you store up the food for the winter season?"

The grasshopper replied, "Truly speaking, I spent all the summer singing songs and that's why I couldn't store anything."

The ant chucked out a smile and remarked, "Then dance the winter away."

The grasshopper pulled a long face and walked away and worked hard afterward.

THIRTY-NINE

Kulang on Goalgoali Island

One day in 1963, in a perilous flood, people in Fangak area were provided with fishing nets because there was no land to cultivate and plant crops on as the flood covered almost all the grounds. Many cattle died as a result of the flood. People made dykes to control their homes from being flooded but to no avail.

The inhabitants suffered for fourteen years from the flood. Kulang decided to go to the river after he received his nets.

"Better staying in water in the river than staying in water at home, my kids." he told his kids one cold flood day.

"We must now pack and go to the river."

The family accepted Kulang's order. He and his wife, Nyachom with their kids left in a small local canoe to the river. In the river, there were water lilies and weeds' roots as the main food. So Kulang and his family were very happy to get enough food in the river as they had wished.

Kulang went to the river in search of fish but was now happy to supplement his catch with water lilies and weed's roots. The fishing nets and some equipment such as twins and hooks that Kulang took with him helped him catch more fish. He was very lucky in the first two weeks in the river as the catch from the river was plenty. He managed to catch a lot of catfish, mudfish as well as tilapia among others.

But the most disturbing thing in the river was the mosquitos, as Kulang's family members did not have mosquito nets. They would enjoy food during the day time and suffer at night from the mosquitoes. One fine evening, Kulang called his kids and talked to them calculatingly selecting his words with wariness.

"My kids," he began. "We better die of hunger with our people at home than to die rich and lonely on this lonely island full of fish and mosquitoes. The antelope says, 'the home is not abandoned because of thirst or hunger.' We must go back home because there is no place like home."

Kulang and his kids left for their land that they dearly missed since the flood controlled it. They, on the way, were badly longing to see it again. On their way, they could imagine the lovely scenes of nature, the fresh air, the hospitable people, and the quite life of Fangak. All these things came to their mind and Nyachom being too emotional bitterly cried for missing their beautiful land.

When the villagers knew that Kulang and his family had come back, they welcomed him and asked him of why he had returned back quickly.

"The river is a very dangerous place, my people," he told the handful of village people who came to welcome him back home. "It has mosquitoes that bite people badly. If one bites the fish with his teeth, the mosquito will unconditionally bite one's buttock from the back." There was laughter when he said that.

"It is like the fish and mosquitoes have signed a joint operation against my family." he concluded. The good people welcomed him again with their usual hospitality.

We better die of hunger with our people at home than to die rich lonely in this lonely island full of fish and mosquitoes.

FORTY

Kulang Wants Nyachom Dead

There was a heavy rain during one of the autumn seasons. It rained a lot and Nyachom could not cook food as the firewood for cooking was soaked in the water.

It was getting dark and Kulang was expecting his food to be given to him in his *Luak*. Nyachom, on the other hand, was afraid of announcing to Kulang the issue that let the food not to be cooked. She did not know what to do because she lacked courage and became hopeless. She wished the rain was to continue heavily till morning so that there could be no chance for Kulang to demand his food. Unfortunately, the rain stopped in the middle of the night.

"Yes! Have you called me, Nyachom?" Kulang said in a loud voice, when no one actually called him.

"No, I didn't call your name, father of my kids." Nyachom fearfully replied. Kulang only wanted Nyachom to notice him.

"*Aywa!*" he shouted again and paused for a long time. "Did you call my name?"

"No! My dear" Nyachom replied for the second time.

"I hate it when someone called my name and later denied it." he said loudly with anger.

After Kulang finally guessed that Nyachom did not prepare any food for him, he became angry and called her. She quietly and amiably came and sat down miserably as if she was going to her grave.

"I have been waiting for years, Nyachom," Kulang said. "When are you bringing my food?" Nyachom had nothing to say now since Kulang claimed to have waited for years and was trembling with anger.

Nyachom, in the other hand was shivering with fear of either getting killed or caned. "The rain prevented me from…" she said and paused with fright.

"From! … what! Nyachom?" Kulang angrily asked while looking for his spears to do away with her.

"The rain prevented me from cooking your food, father of my kids?" she finally disclosed while trembling in fear and was ready to run away to escape death at the hand of Kulang who had no forgiveness when it came to food.

"What!" he said with closed teeth. "I will kill you today, Nyachom."

"Forgive me, father of my kids. I will double the cooking tomorrow morning." Nyachom begged.

"How do you know I will reach tomorrow with this hunger? It is too late, Nyachom." he thundered. "Just die in peace! Even if you compensate me with Kuer-Kolang whose kid is 'Poon', I will not stop killing you."

Kuer-Kulang was believed to be a rich island with fruits, vegetables that grew in all seasons of the year, and had many resources including fish.

Nyachom finally ran out of Kulang's sight and slept in the neighbourhood. Nyachom knew what she always did to please Kulang.

Finally, in the early morning, after Kulang slept without food, Nyachom prepared a big quantity of food and went to Kulang who did not doze even for a minute during the whole night. She first put the food in his sight and greeted him.

"Good morning, father of my kids," she greeted.

"Good morning to you mother of my kids?" he answered politely, seeing his food before him. "How was the night with you dear?"

"It was good, dear." Nyachom replied.

Then he started to eat his food that was given to him by Nyachom before sunrise.

If she had not prepared the food at first, Kulang would have slaughtered her like a goat.

Finally, the lost peace was restored back again in the family and beyond. Kulang took his garden's tools and worked since the problem was solved.

FORTY-ONE

Kulang Befriends a Trickster

There was an Arab trader in South Sudan who was given an alias name of Dhuorwia so the local people to easily pronounce it. Arabs and Englishmen who once stayed in South Sudan were given names of their choices as their Arabic and English names were hard to pronounce.

Dhuorwia was such a trickster who would claim back by all deceptions even in court, whatever he gave to someone before.

Dhuorwia was a trickster, who would claim back by all deceptions, even in court, whatever he had previously given to someone. Many people feared his friendship because of this.

When Kulang heard about him, he told people that he should be taken to the man so that they could be friends.

"Where does he live?" he asked

"In Fangak town." he was told.

"Well," he said. "He must be my good friend."

There was laughter when he pronounced that he needed the trickster to be his friend.

Kulang left Toch for Fangak town to meet the man. When he arrived, he was shown the place of the man. The Arab trader fully accommodated him with cheers as per Sudanese hospitality.

The two chatted through the help of an interpreter. Sometimes, they communicated using the local Nuer language as the Arab man could speak a little Nuer. The Arab man was very delighted to enjoy conversation with Kulang so they became friends. At that point, Kulang now wanted to go back home to Toch.

"*Dhuorwia, Massalama,*" he said in the little Arabic that he knew. "I am going back home, friend."

"*Tamam*, Mr. Kulang," said Dhuorwia with a friendly face and voice. "But wait for me for two minutes."

In less than a minute, Dhuorwia ordered his workers to give two sacks of millet and one sack of sugar to his new friend, Kulang. Kulang was very glad to carry the three sacks home but he knew what he was going to do as he had a good clue about the man that he had just befriended.

When he arrived at his house, he hid the three sacks in a safe place so that they could not get eaten by his family.

After a long time, Dhuorwia arrived at Kulang's home early in the morning at the time he was bringing out his cows from the *Luak* for fresh morning air.

The two greeted each other cheerfully and were served with good food by Nyachom. After they finished their meal, the two friends talked about the wellbeing of their kids. They also talked about different birds and animals in the land.

Kulang told him some Nuer superstition stories where animals were the main characters. Dhuorwia was fond of listening to Nuer folktales so he could learn the language to the fullest. Dhuorwia told him the folktales of the Arab culture but didn't touch the object of his visit until its time arrived by default.

"My friend," Dhuorwia began with broken Nuer language. "When things become worse, a person goes only to the person he trusts the most. And I trust none in this land other than you. My kids are really suffering because of a lack of milk."

"Thank you for trusting only me in the land, my true friend," Kulang said with endorsement on his face and in his eyes. "Your properties are mine and my properties are yours as well."

"There," he continued, pointing to the handful of cows which he had brought out from the *Luak* and could not be less than fifty head of cattle. "Are your cows, select whichever you want. Feel free because you are in your own *Luak*, Gat-Maar".

Dhuorwia selected the fattest cow and became very happy at being given a milking cow by his friend, Kulang. When the man left

Kulang thought of a revenge tactic in the same way the man used to do to whoever he gave anything.

Kulang collected several stones that he would put in a big container in his house right from the morning of the day that the man took the cow. He started his trick by putting in two stones per a day. He would put in two stones every day representing the morning and evening milkings of the cow at his friend's home.

This process went on for three years until he knew that the cow had given birth to two more calves that increased the total of the cows to four. Kulang was now ready to start his long awaited trick to end his friend's behaviour. He counted the stones for a long time and finally got three thousands two hundred and eighty five (3,285) stones.

Kulang left for his friend's home leaving his stones behind in the same safe place with the three sacks of millet and sugar.

"Oh! My friend Kulang," Dhuorwia called with a mouth open of happiness for being visited by his true friend. "How are your kids?"

"They are fine, my friend." Kulang replied.

The two friends were served with food by Dhuorwia's wife and took rest afterward.

"Has Kuan-Cham got married?" asked Dhuorwia.

"Who is Kuan-Cham?" asked Kulang.

"Your elder son." said Dhuorwia. "Oh, you mean Chamkuan. He is very fine but has not married yet. May be next year." Kulang said, and the two friends roared in laughter because Dhuorwia wrongly pronounced Chamkuan's name.

"My friend, Kulang," Dhuorwia said. "What does the name Chamkuan mean?"

"It means 'Eat Food'." Kulang sharply replied.

"…But why have you named a child like that?" Asked Dhuorwia.

"Leave this topic, Gat-Maar." Kulang said. "It is a long story to tell. It can take me ten years to explain it and your lifetime to understand it."

In the evening Kulang disclosed the purpose of his visit. "I have to go back, my friend." he said.

"No, let us take some more days." Dhuorwia, demanded.

"Thank you!" said Kulang. "I have some garden-work waiting for me. We shall arrange a time for us to spend more days in your home next time, my friend. So, the object of my coming is to take back my cows."

"Cow?" asked Dhourwia.

"Cows" corrected Kulang.

"Have you come for the cow that you gave me three years ago?" asked Dhuorwia

"No, I have come for the cows that I gave you three years ago." Kulang corrected again.

The good friends prolonged their conversation on whether they were cows or cow.

Kulang meant the four cows, including those which were born at Dhuorwia's home, but Dhuorwia, on the other hand, wanted Kulang to take only the one cow that he had taken from him.

"Well," said Dhuorwia. "I thought the cow that you gave me was a gift for good like I had once given you two sacks of millet and a sack of sugar. I thought it was a friendly gift but now I am wrong."

"Yes, you are wrong, Gar-guur." confirmed Kulang. "I did not give it to you for good. When you gave me the sacks, you didn't say I should bring them back. And I did not ask you or request them from you. But in the cows' case, you came and begged me when you said your kids were suffering from a lack of milk. So I gave the cows to you for milking purpose only and not for good." Kulang said.

Dhuoriwia, who was talking in singular form 'cow', would not give in to Kulang, who was talking in plural form 'cows' any of the cows. Even if Dhuorwia gave Kulang one cow, Kulang would not receive it but Dhuorwia did not even want to give him a chicken, let alone a cow because of the gifts he had given to Kulang before.

Kulang was lucky as some people had suffered by Dhuorwia's hands in the past. They said that whenever he wanted to take back anything from a person; he would come even if he found someone mourning or burying a dead person in the cemetery. He had once prevented a dead person from being buried because he needed some money from him. He was a callous man but Kulang was lucky because Dhuorwia had come as a begging-friend and not claiming back his belongings directly as he used to do in the past to the villagers and the traders.

Now Kulang knew what to do. He sued the man in the court.

Dhuorwia was called and arrived in the court. Kulang was asked by the head chiefs to narrate his case. He narrated it clearly so that everyone including Dhuorwia, was nodding their heads in understanding and approval. Kulang had said it correctly without missing or adding any part of the story including the three sacks that were given to him.

"Kulang did not miss or add anything." Dhuorwia told the judges when he was told to narrate his case. "Honestly, the cow he had given me three years ago has three calves as we speak. I have no objection on the number. Kulang will take them back on the condition that he gives me back my two millet sacks and a sugar sack that I gave him four years ago."

Dhuorwia, and all the court-listeners, thought Kulang would not find the required food items that he was given four years ago. People thought that even if he was to buy them, he would still suffer inflation in the market because of the price's yearly increase.

"No problem I will try my best." Kulang said. The judges gave Kulang and Dhuorwia two days for them to bring the sacks and the cows to be exchanged between them in the court.

The two left the court room while Dhuorwia was smiling as he had never lost any case before in court. He doubted that Kulang could find sugar even if he managed to get the millet because he was the only trader selling sugar in the land. He was even ready to give the cows back to Kulang in case Kulang, by a miracle got the sacks from nowhere.

After two days, the two returned and sat down before the judges with the four cows and three sacks and a container full of stones. Everyone wondered why Kulang brought stones with him when he was only told to bring the needed sacks.

"Dhuorwia," the judge called out, "are these three sacks yours?"

"Yes, they are the same. Mine with the dots I had put on each sack," he replied.

"Kulang" he was called, "could these cows be yours?"

"Yes they are." he said. "I know their line despite the fact that some were born in exile."

The judge told their servants to exchange the cows and sacks between the two friends.

As the case was going to be finalized, Kulang asked to speak again.

"You are welcome." he was told by one of the chiefs.

"Thank you, Kuar," he said politely. "Now the judgment is fair and transparent but there is one thing that we have not solved."

"Everything is solved, Kulang." cried another senior chief.

"Sir, the milk case is not solved." he said calmly and graciously. "Dhuorwia has been milking my cows for three years and I have stored his sacks for four years. Look at this container; each stone represents the milk of my cow that he has been milking on a daily basis for three years. Am I not the victim now here?"

At that point, everybody was convinced and Dhuorwia was told to defend himself but all he could do was to no avail. Thus, the court asked Dhuorwia to compensate Kulang's milk of three years.

Dhuorwia had to give his shop away for he could not get jailed and decided to go to Malakal town to bring money but he never returned again. Kulang had saved the people from a trickster.

"This world is confusing." Kulang told the court-listeners. "When you treat someone the same why he treats you, he gets upset and angry. My friend Dhuorwia has been treating people badly but when I imitated his behaviour, he became unhappy and maybe he is insulting me now in his mind calling me bad names but I do not care since I don't hear the insults."

Kulang Befriends a Trickster

*Dhuorwia has been milking my cows for three years
and I have stored his sacks for four years.*

"There are many ways to fight the enemy." he jokingly told the people in his village when he left the court. "But what matters is to defeat the enemy with logic like I did. When one uses logic and facts, God also uses logics and facts. But when one tells lies, God also tells lies."

FORTY-TWO

Kulang Regrets Chasing Nyachom Away

One day Kulang had a heated argument with his wife, Nyachom, over the continuous coming of visitors which he blamed on her.

"Nyachom," Kulang angrily called as they were blaming one another. "Please tell the visitors not to come again."

"It is up to you to stop them, Kulang." Nyachom said calmly. "The visitors come because of you."

"How?" asked Kulang while glaring at her but Nyachom ignored his enquiry to avoid getting badly caned.

The war of words between the two couples escalated and Kulang finally concluded it by telling his wife to go back to her parents' home.

"Leave my home immediately or prepare to lose a tooth, Nyachom." he said heatedly, pointing at Nyachom with his shaking index-finger. "You have no use in my life. You have been wasting my resources by giving them to your visitors. Move as soon as possible before I send you to your grave."

As soon as Nyachom learnt that she was told to leave with an immediate ultimatum by her husband, she began to collect her things so that she could go. When she finished collecting her belongings, she called her first-born daughter for instructions regarding the services she should do in the house while she was away.

"My daughter, take good care of your dad," she told her daughter.

Kulang left what he was doing and stood still like an old Nim tree, listening attentively to their conversation.

"Anytime he comes from the garden-work, give him his water with his big cup and always give him cooked beans before any food as an appetizer and then make his soup hot at noon time."

"But," she continued. "Take care of visitors. Don't give what belongs to your father to visitors."

Kulang in surprise seriously looked at Nyachom with reducing irritation.

"Nyachom," he respectfully called from where he stood. "Won't all the good things you have said confuse the child, my dear? I am afraid she will get confused as she will not do them as you always do."

"No, she will not," answered Nyachom sharply. "This girl is so knowledgeable. She resembles me not you."

At that point, Kulang was left with no choice as Nyachom was about to go and he feared the kid might not do as well as Nyachom used to do.

"You can just go and come." he said with eyes turned down in embarrassment. "But how long will you spend there?"

"I don't know," replied Nyachom uninterested. "Because I don't go at my wish, you chased me. I may not come back again, maybe forever because my father shall return you some cows when the marriage contract is broken soon."

"What are you talking about, Nyachom?" he said with eyes popped out. "What brings all this now? Could all this be the results of the little love and fun arguments we have recently made?"

"If it is the case," he continued. "Then, two of us shall depart and leave. Who has no family among us? My mother, Nyadoak Kier, and my father, Toat Kang, are alive. I must also pack and go and stay with them. I thought you were just going to visit your relatives."

Nyachom finally was moved to pity her husband who was talking sadly in hopelessness. She then changed her mind and unpacked the already packed luggage.

Kulang became extremely happy to see Nyachom back to her normal duties.

FORTY-THREE

Kulang Chases Away Nyachom's Sister

One day, Kulang's sister-in-law and her two small children, a boy and a girl, arrived at home and were fully accommodated by Nyachom. Kulang was knitting cattle's robes while Nyachom prepared everything for the visitors.

He became annoyed with Nyachom and the visitors but didn't say anything or let them know. It was harvesting season when millet was to be harvested. Everyone was busy in their fields.

The next day, early in the morning, Kulang left for his garden work and the two women, Nyachom and her sister who had arrived the previous night, went with him to the field to help him. The work was always made easy with songs by the farmers for it to be finished as quickly as they could in order to do away with boredom. The three workers started their work very well and harvested enough crops.

It was now noon time when the sun had reached the middle of the sky and their shadows faded away unlike the morning when they all had long shadows. The heat rained down on the three workers, Kulang, Nyachom and her sister. It was like the breath of hell. As they were going to the final point when the sun was getting hotter, Kulang started a song that made the two women go silent.

"*Lhak mi jiak mi ci Kuoth-Nhial e nonga theen,*" crooned Kulang in a song that he suddenly created. "*chatke mi cha chiek nak kel ke gaat-ke dang rew, nyal kene dhol. Chi nger a nger kor, eey cha tem piny cha tuolka kuay. Tuolka han Gat-Toat.*" which literally means 'I had a terrible dream last night like I had killed a woman with her two children, a boy and a girl. This harvesting will turn to fight if people don't respect the son of Toat.'

Nyachom paid a great attention to the song which was sung by her husband, Kulang. Her sister didn't pay any attention to the song as she had never expected that her sister's husband would hate her and her kids.

When they arrived home Nyachom called her sister and told her the lyrics of the song which Kulang had sung during their work in the garden.

"For your safety," Nyachom said to her sister. "Your kids' as well as my safety, pack and go, sister. We shall meet in the name of the God of our ancestors."

The girl left with her kids, boy and girl, and Kulang became happy at Nyachom's quick understanding.

FORTY-FOUR

Kulang Rejects Ghost Marriage

Ghost marriage is a marriage that takes place on the behalf of a dead relative in order to beget children in his name. It is also a marriage where a deceased groom is replaced by his brother or another relative that is not an uncle, son or father to the deceased. Marriage to the dead person among the Nuer is as equal as the marriage to a live man.

One morning at just some minutes before lunch time, some old men arrived at Kulang's home. Nyachom was going to take the food to her husband had she not seen the visitors. Kulang knew from the faces of the visitors that they had come to tell troubling news but he did not ask them. He welcomed them cheerfully and they sent for Nyachom as they needed her to share the meeting with them.

"Cousins," Kulang called them. "Tell me the agenda of the meeting first before Nyachom is called. If it is an announcement of a death then leave it for next time as people have not yet eaten and Nyachom is too emotional when it comes to bereavement. I did not eat some years ago when one of the idiots of this land disclosed her brother's death before the meal."

"No," said one of the old men. "We have not come to announce someone's death here, Gat-Toat?"

"Well," he said. "Let us continue then. Let her come."

Nyachom was called and sat respectfully looking down to avoid the men' eyes as per the custom. She thought deeply in fear that someone might have died as Nuer elder say 'The heart is evil'. When one has a relative in a distance place sometimes the heart kills him while he is still alive.

"Well, it has been a long time since we met." said one of the men to Nyachom but her heart was still beating before the agenda was disclosed. "It is always good for an old woman like you to be included in family meetings."

Nyachom thanked them but was still worried badly and guessed the death of many of her relatives but she was wrong. Kulang was the only happiest person in the Luak since he was assured that their coming would not stop people from eating.

"We can now start our meeting." said the second man and waved to his neighbour to start the meeting's agenda.

"Well," the shortest man of all cleared his throat. "I had a dream last night and I decided to tell you here in your home. That is the reason why many of us have come."

Nyachom was finally relieved when she heard the agenda was about a dream.

"Dream!" Kulang astoundingly asked.

"Yes, a dream," he was told.

Kulang would have nearly chased away the men had it not been for his respect for an old man who came with them.

"Why would you come all the way from your homes and stop my wife from doing her morning work just to tell us a dream?" Kulang asked, while turning his head away in fury.

"Listen to it first. Maybe it will make sense because it is not just a dream but a dream with meaning." said the oldest of the men that Kulang respected. He told the owner of the dream to reveal his dream.

"Kulang," he called out with a clear voice. "Your late brother came to me in a dream."

"Came to you? Where is he?" Kulang asked in disbelief.

"Not physically but in a dream at night. He came in a dream and this is what he told me: 'My dear, failure to convey this message to my dear brother Kulang Toat will have consequences for you and your family members. Tell Kulang to marry a wife for me as soon as possible or I do what suits me if he needs the two of us to have no children on earth. It is now the third year since I died and Kulang has not married for me.' That was the message of your late brother?" the man stopped as he let his companions explain more on the consequences of ignoring dead people's messages.

Now all the men talked to Kulang to convince him to prepare urgently for this marriage as needed. Kulang did not listen to the words of the speakers as he was busy picturing the message and he talked while stopping the last speaker before finalizing his speech.

"Well," Kulang exclaimed. "Lucky me! I have been trying in vain to get my late brother and my dead relatives who have died. But now someone has met my dead brother easily." There was silence as the men thought Kulang was going to thank them for their coming but they were wrong.

"Now, if you, the owner of the dream," he continued. "can talk to dead people, and then I want you to ask him the whereabouts of the two cows that he took before he died. Ask him also to talk to our two dead in-laws who didn't complete paying the dowries of our sisters who are now depending on me. Ask him if he had collected our cows and goats that died the following years. Let him correspondingly ask Toat Kang about his grandfather's nickname. Now tell me the replies before I comment on your dream's marriage."

There was silence in the *Luak*. Nobody had a courageous heart to reply Kulang's questions not even Nyachom. When he knew there was silence and the time for his food had arrived, he talked angrily wanting the men to leave.

"Am I not talking to people? Or you have no ears? Or you have come to mock me on my brother's death? You, the owner of the dream, sleep now and talk to my brother before it is too late." The dream owner was still silent. But the oldest man who saw anger in Kulang's face convinced him quietly by calling him with his good names.

"Gatdila," he said. "The dream comes alone. Nobody can intend to dream."

"No, he must dream again," Kulang said crossly, threatening the dream owner to sleep during the daytime so that he could talk to the dead people he mentioned. "The same way he had it, he must have it any time. I am ready to give him a sleeping mat, bed sheet and pillow if he thinks his house is too far."

Kulang stood up and turned to Nyachom but said nothing. Nyachom understood his body language and was seen going toward the direction of her hut. She left to prepare the lunch as she knew Kulang would chase the visitors by all means necessary.

"Listen," he said in an ostentatious voice. "There is nothing called 'Ghost marriage' in this world. It is a waste of scarce resources. Why would a dead person demand a family when he died already? Why do you men of this land give the highest consideration to the messages of dead people leaving and ignore the messages of the people still alive? Whenever I say we should all work in our gardens and stop random visitation, no one listens. Are you waiting for my death in order for you to implement my important messages? Now if you have come to mock me in my home because of my brother's death then remain in your places here." he said.

Upon hearing that, the men speedily left as Kulang would fight them if they failed to implement the order.

Nyachom at last put the well-cooked lunch before Kulang who enjoyed his food which was nearly eaten in the name of a dream.

Kulang lived long and nothing happened to him and his family when he failed to marry for his late brother as per the old men's recommendation.

"People should stop wasting scare resources by marrying people to the dead when many unmarried young energetic men are there wanting wives. People who love the dead should name their children after the dead people's names instead of marrying for them."

FORTY-FIVE

Kulang Betrays his Family

One fine morning, Kulang and his family members left for a distant village far away. They became very tired and were exhausted by their thirst and hunger on the way. They decided to take rest at a nearby homestead along the road as it was hard for their legs to carry them ahead.

When they rested, the owner of the home that they had rested at accommodated them with a dish full of food. Kulang as well as Nyachom knew that the food would not satisfy the family so he employed tactics that later victimized the kids.

"My kids," he called out quietly in a fatherly expression after he saw the kids were desperately and hungrily looking as if to say 'the food is little'. "This food is not very little for us. It will satisfy all of us if we eat it strategically with cold hearts."

"How will it be eaten strategically with cold hearts?" asked Nyachom. "We must only let the kids eat it and two of us shall remain until God gives us food because stomach is the God's plate."

"Aha! You have ears and you don't understand," he loudly laughed with forced mirth.

"It's unfair, Nyachom. Did you come to an agreement with God that He will give us food later? Now I have a very fair and decent plan for us to eat this food. Let us all line up since we are one family. The head must be the head and the second one must follow and so forth until the last junior." Nyachom kept silent because she was, with a hungry voice, rebuked by Kulang when she said the food should be given to the kids.

Kulang convinced his wife that God didn't give food but health. "If God gave food to people for free, there would be no poor and rich. God only gives health and it is up to the owner of the health to transform it into wealth through hard work or into begging and visiting homes in the name of relations."

In acceptance of Kulang's suggestion, now there was a long line with Kulang leading it and Nyachom following and so on, one child after the other in the order of who was first born.

"What next now that that we have lined up?" asked Nyachom.

"Well, these spoons," he said clearing his throat with the plate in front of him and pointing at the spoons which were brought for each of them. "have no use anymore; one spoon is enough because we must eat this food with one mouth for it will reach everyone's stomach equally. My mouth is the family's mouth. Therefore it is our mouth. So is my stomach. The food will reach all of us if I eat it first."

Kulang started to eat whereas Nyachom and her kids at his back in a long line were expecting food to reach them as per their father's remark.

"Has it arrived?" Kulang asked them after he swallowed a big quota of food.

"No!" all the family members said miserably as their legs were too tired to allow them to stand for so long.

Kulang Betrays his Family

Kulang started to eat whereas Nyachom and her kids at his back in a long line were expecting food to reach them as per their father's remark.

"Well, it is on the way, my kids. Just wait," he told them while continuing to eat with his big spoon. The kids waited thinking that the food would reach them but to no avail. Any time he asked them whether it had arrived he was told that it didn't. The line remained standing for some few minutes until Kulang finished the food leaving his poor children hungry.

"That is how people with different mothers behave," he silently said to himself while enjoying satisfaction. "The truth is only told to specific people in this world."

FORTY-SIX

Kulang's Broken Promise

It was a cold morning day when Kulang called Nyachom and requested food and drink.

"Where is my food and drink?" he asked.

"Oh, father of my kids." she replied respectfully. "Isn't it too early for you to eat or drink something?"

"Okay Nyachom," he said, clearing his throat. "And what time do throats open?"

Nyachom could not answer that very tough question and instead ran to the kitchen and served Kulang with well-cooked food that she had urgently cooked. Kulang became fully satisfied and happy when he finished his food which was given to him in the early morning.

Shortly, after he finished, Nyachom returned to take back the utensils as usual but he stopped her as she was going back to her hut with the dish in her hand.

"Nyachom, stop," he called, and Nyachom stood still.

"How many times have we eaten since we came into the face of this world."

Nyachom was surprised but managed to answer him.

"It cannot be counted." she simply replied.

"Well," he said. "Then if it cannot be counted as you said, why don't we stop eating to see the other side of life without food so that we know the experience?"

Nyachom gave a beautiful smile but said nothing.

"Tell me your view on that." he demanded. "Don't you know that you are tired of daily cooking and both of us are tired of continuous eating in this world, mother of my kids?"

"I don't think it will be possible for a human being to continue living without food." Nyachom said, looking at him with womanly sweet eyes.

"No, it will be possible, Nyachom." he replied sharply. "But why is life possible while we have been eating for so long? The same way we have been eating and still alive is the same way we shall be living for the rest of our life without eating."

"Well I agree." Nyachom promised but with secret reservations. Nyachom agreed outwardly as she gave a sign of endorsement in front of Kulang but inwardly she was not.

"Okay thank you, mother of my kids." he said with serious voice as if he had been tired of eating for so long. "Go and don't cook again for the rest of your life please. Give away everything we have to the food lovers of this land. But be careful not give them to the lazy food lovers. Give them to the hardworking food lovers because they deserve them."

Nyachom left but didn't give away their things as demanded by Kulang because she knew the consequences would be on her neck at the end of the game. She instead secretly prepared the evening meal and put it somewhere out of reach in the house.

Morning and afternoon had now gone away while Kulang was still in his promise of not eating for the rest of his life. Now the sun was slowly fading away and Kulang was little by little realizing some change in his stomach though the promise was still intact. The morning satisfaction was now going away against all his expectations. Kulang finally became hungry before the day was over. But what was he going to do now since he had promised not to eat again for his entire lifetime and he had ordered Nyachom to give away everything? Kulang always wanted people dead when he was hungry.

Now he looked around excruciatingly toward Nyachom's hut and he could not see smoke as usual. Nyachom was resting with her head on her palm and she was innocently looking away to avoid Kulang's eyes. Perhaps she was thinking about the outcome of the promise that she had never crossed or heard in her entire life.

Kulang didn't know what to do and he tried to find reasons against Nyachom but all to no avail because Nyachom decided not to give him a chance on something that he himself had sworn.

Kulang saw Nyachom looking away when he came and asked her. "Nyachom, what are you looking at now?" he said furiously.

"Nothing, father of my kids," she simply answered while turning her eyes away as she knew Kulang was very hungry.

"There is nothing called 'nothing' in this world, Nyame," he angrily said. "You better tell me now." At that moment Kulang had found a reason to fight Nyachom because he had been longing for a reason to do so but to no avail.

"Okay, I am just looking at that beautiful forest in our village." Nyachom said with a smile, pointing at the nearby forest.

"What?" he shouted. "Then why are you looking at it for a long time? Are you mad? What has it done to you? Do you think the forest has no person to fight you? Okay wait for me, stupid woman. I have now taken the side of the forest." Kulang quickly and hungrily went to his *Luak* crooning with the war song and brought out his spears and other weapons to kill Nyachom for looking at the village's forest.

Nyachom did not take long as she speedily ran to her hut and brought out the food when she knew Kulang was going to kill her.

"Here is your food, father of my kids." said Nyachom, kneeling down before Kulang who had spears in his hand.

"Thank you, my beautiful wife." he said, putting down his spears and other weapons.

Kulang ate until he became fully satisfied and returned to his consciousness. He thought for a while and called Nyachom again. "It is now your choice, my dear wife." he said." To look back at your good-looking forest or not." Nyachom said nothing but went away taking the empty dish to her hut.

After a long thought again, he called her and she came and sat before him.

"Life is about trying new things," he began," I hate people who don't try new things for experience. It is not good living your life with other people's experience. Better first-hand experience than the second hand one. If we had not tried the hunger, we wouldn't have known it. We have now without doubts known that, life without food is very dangerous. It needs hard work to avoid the hunger and also the disabled people who are hungry should be helped but not those lazy people with hands, legs and eyes."

All this happened just between sun rise and sun set.

FORTY-SEVEN

Relocation inside the Hut

Nyachom decided to clean Kulang's grass thatched hut one day and she wanted him to relocate to the other side of the hut which she had cleaned at first because she did not want him go outside.

"Father of my kids," she began. "I want to clean this side now. You can relocate to the other side so that you come back soon when I finished cleaning."

"Okay, mother of my kids." he said. "But what have you done so far concerning this journey?"

"Which journey?" Nyachom demanded.

"Okay," he cleared his throat. "Honestly, there is no short or long journey if it comes to leaving one place for another. For that reason, you must first cook a very big meal and prepare some drink so that I start my journey to the new destination that you want me to go to. No matter how long or short the journey is, the mean for reaching there is the same. There must be something to be eaten on the way. I know you think it is not a journey but we are different people with different thoughts."

Nyachom now knew that she would not clean her husband's hut's side unless she fulfilled his demand. She at first just wanted to sweep the part of the hut and her husband to just relocate to the other side of it but now there was a condition. But she really loved him so much under all odds and now she knew what she was going to do in order for her husband to stay in an arranged place. She went back to the kitchen and doubled the morning meal with another delicious food and knelt down before him.

"Yes," Kulang happily said. "This is how someone can be told to relocate even if it means going to the end of the world. Now I have to go and eat at the end of the journey." He stretched his hands and carried his food to the other side of the hut that he considered to be the new destination.

Finally, his hut was put to a well-ordered environment and he returned shortly. "Thank God I am back in peace from the journey," he flippantly said to Nyachom who was busy collecting utensils. "The journey should be treated with respect and care for a safe arrival."

FORTY-EIGHT

The Fight over the Grassland

Cattle to the Nuer are the sources of milk, food, dowry as well as settling disputes. Cattle also provide the manure/dung used for making fire. All the Nuer cattle are grass-fed. They eat bluegrass, ryegrass, Bermuda grass, and fescue among other grasses in the forest.

Kulang's village youth had a quarrel with their neighbouring clan over the best remaining grassland since most of the grasslands were either eaten up by cattle or burnt down by the wildfire. The two clans could not reach a peaceful agreement. They decided to fight and fixed a day for them to fight.

'Fighting', according to the Nuer culture of war, is announced so the warring sides can prepare themselves by informing their members far away from them and arming themselves with their weapons. Now the days had passed and people were going to fight in two days' time.

When the two days had passed, the youth grouped themselves for the battle ahead. As the youth started march to the battle against the other clan, Kulang approached hundreds of his clan men.

"My sons," he told them. "I see your morale is high, are you going to help the Anyanya fight the Arabs?"

"No," one of the angry youth told him. "Our neighbouring clan does not know our masculinity and bravery in this land; they have for three days now been letting their cattle graze in the only grassland where our cattle get their pasture."

"Fight for cattle?" Kulang asked in astonishment. "It is going to be an unjust war. It is going to be unfair to fight over the grassland for cattle when cattle themselves are alive and sound. The cattle should be the ones to fight not human beings since they are the first beneficiaries of that grassland. I want you now to go back to your homes and leave the fight for our cattle against the cattle of our neighbouring clan. Real men fight only a just war and not an unjust one. Only a grass eater among you will be involved in the upcoming fight since it will be his right to fight for the sake of his food. Do you have any cows among you as we are talking." The angry youth didn't listen to Kulang's advice and instead left toward the battlefield.

"Well," exclaimed Kulang, who got disappointed when the youth abandoned him before he finished his speech. "These young men lack reasoning." he said to himself. "They will be the victims at the end of the fight because an unjust war has consequences whether defeated or defeating. Our strong men, the Anyanya, have been fighting the Arabs in the watch of the cattle without their reinforcement. Now our men want to be involved in a supposed cattle versus cattle war when none of the cattle are involved in our war. What a fake people?"

The war had now stopped in favour of his clan-men who defeated the enemy but lost one of their men leaving the enemy without death but serious casualties. His clan youth, as they returned, were very happy singing local ground-breaking songs for winning the battle.

Kulang approached them again.

"Tell me how the battle was." Kulang demanded.

"It was the real men's fight against the women in form of men." said a young man who was the group's lead singer. "We defeated and dislodged the cowards but we have lost one hero in our side."

"What?" Kulang asked shockingly. "Did you say you lost one of your men? Now what is the benefit of defeating the enemy if you lost a person? Did you bring home the grass land? Being defeated by an enemy with fewer casualties inflicted on your side is better than defeating an enemy with more casualties inflicted on your side."

FORTY-NINE

The Lazy Neighbour

The first rain of the autumn season had been heavy and it was not the rain of planting season. People still waited for the third rain so that the soil was well softened.

One of Kulang's neighbours was a lethargic person. He had some disturbing traits in avoiding work so it would be done by his wife. Whenever he noticed that only a few days were left for the planting time, he would travel far away with the pretense of visiting relatives in the other villages, only to return when he knew his wife had finished everything.

There was this year when it rained heavily and the planting of the seeds was expected in a few days. He was believed to only get up by the cock's crow otherwise no one in the house would tell him to get up.

Kulang had, during one village gathering-day, insulted him in parable when they were chatting after they had drunk their wine.

"Lazy people and those young people who have hard time waking up in the morning use the cock's crow to wake them up rather than the natural morning rush-hour traffic." said Kulang while many were listening. "There is no problem with that as long as they do their work after they are awoken by a rooster. But my fear is the time when the cock is slaughtered for food or when it is eaten by cats. I believe the lazy people will spend the rest of their life sleeping because no cock will wake them up."

The man knew that Kulang had wisely attacked him but he said nothing and none of the gatherers commented on Kulang's dry topic since it could lead to a fight. They finally dispersed peacefully when they had finished their wine.

When Kulang's neighbour reached his home, he called his wife and assured her that he was going to visit his sick friend in a distant village. The man did that because he wanted to avoid the work so it was done by his poor wife. The poor wife unconditionally accepted the request of her husband as per the culture.

It was now only a few days left for the heavy rain to come when the villagers would plant their gardens. Everyone was happily looking forward to the day. Like the villagers, the poor wife had also been happily waiting for the planting day as she had already leveled the garden. Finally, the rain poured down and it was the rain for the planting time. All the people went to their gardens the next day to plant their crops.

Unfortunately, the wife became severely sick and could not plant her garden with the villagers together and nobody had noticed that she was sick because her kids were too young to inform the neighbours and the villagers.

Kulang had different thoughts at night on the failure of his neighbour to plant his garden. Kulang did not know that the man had left and he didn't know that the wife was sick too.

"Oh!" he loudly said at night. "It is now the third day when everyone as well as me planted crops. And that neighbour of mine has not yet planted anything. Is he indeed punishing me for the insult of that day when we drank wine together? If he really means to punish me by not planting his garden, I believe my family will be in trouble in future when harvesting comes. To avoid future inconvenience I must secretly go and plant seeds in their garden."

Kulang jumped to his feet, took his planting stick for digging the earth, and brought out from his pot millet-seeds that he had saved from the previous harvest; maize, groundnut, sesame and all other crops that his neighbour might need when harvesting commenced. He directly went at night towards his neighbour's garden.

Kulang started planting his neighbour's field to make sure they had crops to harvest should the harvesting season pass so that the neighbour would not be reliant to him and his family.

He planted it the whole night and returned to sleep at the cock's crow. Kulang didn't tell anybody including his wife that he had planted his neighbour's garden. He helped plant his neighbour's garden secretly not in kind-heartedness but for the safety of his family when harvesting came.

In the Nuer culture, neighbours share many things in common and that might be the reason that made Kulang plant his neighbour's field at night. Five days after he had planted the garden of his neighbour, the poor wife recovered only to find out that her vast garden was planted by an unidentified person.

But Kulang could not tell them that he was the one. The wife thought it might be a miracle as she could not find the person. The lazy husband had to arrive only after he knew all the work was no more in the garden. Now he had returned and would go back again in the middle of the rainy season when removal of weeds started. Kulang's neighbour had many harvests at the end of the season and they did not ask anything from his family. That made Kulang very happy indeed as no one disturbed him in his home.

Kulang was now ready to deal only with the visitors after he solved his neighbour's problem. He wished he could make the visitors work hard and stop visiting other people for accommodation. It would have been very tough to him in dealing with people on both the fronts, his neighbours' and the visitors' at the same time. He had now made himself ready to accommodate the visitors .

"A next door neighbour's problem can turn to be the other neighbour's problem in the long run." Kulang told the villagers one day without explaining more. The people could not understand what Kulang was up to. Kulang wanted to tell them that if someone was facing difficulties, all of the people around that person would be at risk. He wanted the villagers to help and encourage one another and not to leave anyone with his problems.

FIFTY

The Death of Kulang

On September 1st 1968, Kulang, the ground-breaking man of the land, lay on his death papyrus-mat waiting for his final demise. All the family members including the neighbours surrounded him as it is a custom for the Nuer people to listen to a dying person en masse hoping to receive a consecrated word for one's life. Everybody as well as Kulang, knew without doubt that he was going to die because old age had consumed him.

Kulang tilled in his garden the day before his death. He was a strong man who liked work.

"Nyachom!" he called painfully followed by cough. "My ancestors and friends are waiting for me. I will join them today." he paused for a while as some kids were crying.

"Why are the kids crying?" he asked. "Stop crying! It is not worth crying for an old person who has eaten all types of food of this world. Cry only for the little ones who have not yet enjoyed the good life of the world. An old man doesn't die but falls. Our fathers say an old man 'has fallen'…But, there is one thing that disturbs me a lot; I am afraid there will be no person like Nyachom, in the world of the dead to help me. It will only be good if I die this morning and Nyachom follows in the evening."

There was silence around, including Nyachom, as she did not want to die. Because people feared the words of a dying person, there was no one brave enough to counter Kulang's dishonest demand in wanting Nyachom dead.

Kulang went on talking to people around his death-mat. He told his children to take good care of his black cow's descendants as they would help them.

He then turned to the kids and said: "I see that I am the unluckiest one. It appears in your faces that there will be no death again, and you look like you will have an everlasting life. I see that people will fool around, enjoy and waste their times one day to avoid work above in that blue sky with their loved ones who are far away from them.

"Well, I do not know more about the everlasting life but take this message from me. You boys and girls, go to school. School brings sweet things like sugar and many things that will come ahead. River, land and sky ships will be produced by school. Go and study well, my offspring." he paused for a long while.

A second or two later, Kulang slowly turned his head to the right, and got the most horrific look on his face as if he was eyeing at something the masses couldn't see and depressed, his face knotted, and he screamed. People actually thought that Kulang had died right then and there but he woke a few moments later by opening his eyes and continued.

"My dear children, I want all of you to work hard and encourage one another. Your cheering words can lift someone up and help them to make it through the day. But your negative words can

The Death of Kulang

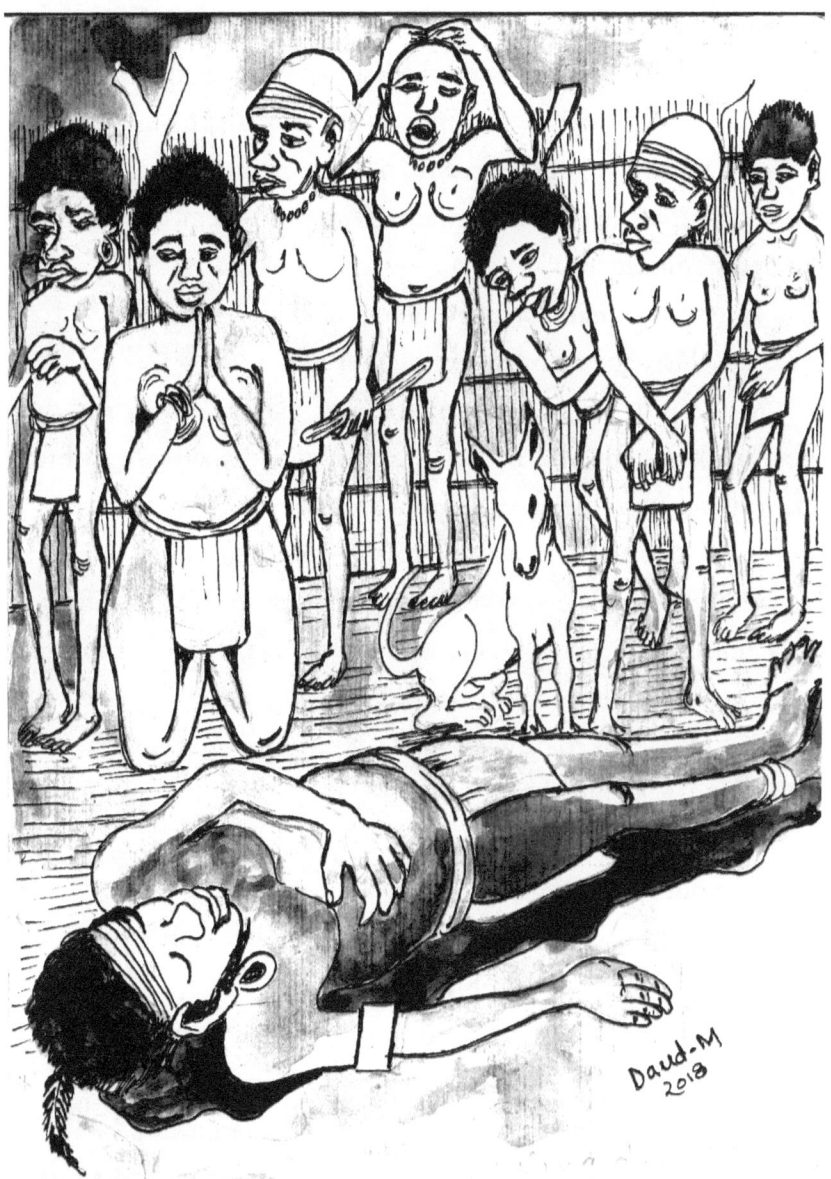

Stop crying! It is not worth crying for an old person who has eaten all types of food of this world. Cry only for the little ones who have not yet enjoyed the good life of the world.

cause deep wounds; they may be the spears that destroy someone's desire to continue trying or even their existence on the face of the world. Your destructive and impromptu words can surely reduce someone in the eyes of the crowds, destroy their influence and have a lasting impact on the way others respond to them. Be careful of the detestation speech!"

"Where are Chamkuan and Duer," he demanded. The two boys walked to his sight with tears in their eyes.

"My sons, I am an old man who has lived in this world than everyone here. For that matter I have a good experience of life. I am very happy to die at this age in front of you. It is always good for an old man to be buried by his son than a son to be buried by his father. A forehead-marked Wut is responsible for the effect of his actions. If the action was based on kindness, it would churn out only kindness in the long run. If the action has been wickedness, the outcome also tends to be wickedness. Now my garden and the tools for tilling are happily dancing because I am dying. It is up to you to continue the fight on or give up because they are mocking me as if you were not men to revenge."

He then turned to the people around him and said: "You people, if you wish to be feared in life join the army right from now, but if you wish to be respected in life work hard in your gardens. The world respects only those with resources and fears those with military uniforms and guns. The choice is yours now; to be feared or respected. You are all here around my death-mat not because I treated you well before but because I have been a strong worker. Even those whom I have never given a sack of maize in my life respect me because of the resources I have had. To be honest and clear with you; if you are very kind, honest, friendly and poor at the same time, believe me nobody would laugh even if you told the funniest joke in the land."

Finally, Kulang waved goodbye to the mourners and closed his eyes for the last time and his family waved him the last goodbye too. He was put to rest in his farmhouse at Toch in Fangak.

FIFTY-ONE

The Death of Nyachom

The sun was up and lively over a clear, light blue sky. It was now time to say goodbye to the strongest and unshakable woman in the whole world as she was going to start her journey toward death. People could not help but felt encouraged by her encouraging words. Nyachom, despite the coup she had made against her elder sister, Nyalora, more than fifty years before or so, was still the best wife in the universe.

Like her husband Kulang, she had been a hard-working woman who always stayed attentive to the tasks in her house and beyond. Her work had been consistently judged as of acceptable to excellent quality by all the people in the land, and she looked for more work if everything that was assigned to her by Kulang was done. No matter how hard the job given to her by Kulang, she would do it in an excellent way. She had never gotten tired of Kulang's noises for over fifty years staying with him. God might have purposely meant sending her to Kulang, the sturdiest man in the whole world.

Regardless of the suffering she had undergone in most parts of her life, she was still greatly in love with her husband, alive or dead. As a matter of fact, the woman who can do as Nyachom is not yet born and I am afraid she will never be born again due to the fact that she survived a million death threats from her husband.

When Nyachom knew of her natural end, she called together her broods and relations and told them to be kind and good to one another.

"Life is very short," she said with a forced smile on her dying face to comfort the young ones. "You must love one another. I want my daughters to respect their husbands as the custom demands. The more one respects, trusts and loves her husband with all her heart the more years she will spend on earth just like my husband and I spent. Our ancestors say 'better an avaricious husband than an avaricious wife'. Also take good care of your mothers and fathers in-law. The wives who are not well brought up by their families always disclaim their mothers' in-law and want their husband to choose them over their mothers. A mother or father in-law from both sides deserves respect, love and appreciation for making a wife or husband marriageable. All the bad women should not be quick to forget that they are potential mothers-in-law, and that whatever they sow as daughters-in-law today, they will reap it when they become mothers-in-law. Parents' in-law should be loved before the old age consumes them. They should not be treated as rivals or enemies." she paused and thought for a long time.

"What do I need again if I have all these wonderful and strong people around me?" she said with a smile while on her death-mat. "Actually I feel much buoyed up emotionally."

Nyachom did not die in the evening of the September 1st 1968 as Kulang wished. Nyachom lived another more years before she

*My death will give chance to the coming generation
like our ancestors gave chances to us.*

could follow him in 1970. Nyachom died a peaceful death just like her husband.

"I need no one to weep." she continued as she felt her final departure. "I have not died young but at my natural end. Nothing lasts forever. My death will give way to the coming generation like our ancestors gave way to us."

Nyachom had lived with her husband Kulang for over fifty years with many bitter and moral experiences. Nyachom Loang now closed her eyes for the last time and followed her husband who had died two years before her. She was put to rest just near the tomb of her late husband, Kulang.

Teaching resources

Kulang Toat Kang
1. Where and when was Kulang Toat Kang born?
2. Which tribe does he belong to in South Sudan?
3. How many dogs did Kulang have? Name them.
4. What is the name of Kulang's mother?
5. When and where did Kulang die?
6. What do Kulang's two dogs' names (Ken-Thiengdak and Guichi Ha Ngu) mean?
7. What do Kulang's two sons' names (Chamkuan and Duer) mean?

Chapter 1
1. Who did Kulang propose to marry at first?
2. What happened when Kulang proposed to Nyalora?
3. In which season did Kulang return to his in-laws?
4. Who did Kulang see when he reached his in-law's house?
5. Who was among the playing kids?
6. What did Kulang do when he saw the kids?
7. What happened to the kids when they heard the voice but could not see the caller?
8. Did Nyachom run with the kids?
9. What did Kulang tell Nyachom when he revealed himself to her?
10. How did Nyachom reply to Kulang?
11. What were Kulang's two demands when he revealed himself to Nyachom?
12. What did Nyachom promise Kulang?
13. In the evening, the father of the girls called his daughters for a brief meeting. What was the meeting's agenda about?
14. What did Nyalora, Nyachom and other cousins do at night?
15. Who napped during the cooking process, and why did Nyachom assure them to take rest?
16. What did Nyachom do after the girls were sound asleep?

17. What happened to the fish in the morning?
18. What did the mother and her boys attempt to do?
19. What was their father's advice?
20. A month later, Kulang returned to his in laws' home. Who did he see again and what did he do?
21. Why did the kids run and what did Kulang tell Nyachom again?
22. Why did Nyachom break the milk-gourd?
23. What had the youth nearly done to the dog? Why?
24. What did their father say?
25. Who came to *Luak* with Kulang during the marriage haggling?
26. What did Kulang say when he started to talk inside the *Luak*?
27. How did the father of Nyalora and Nyachom answer Kulang?
28. What was the reaction inside the *Luak* when Kulang changed his mind from Nyalora?
29. Why did Kulang decide to change his mind?
30. What did the girls' father say at last?
31. What did the girls' uncle say?
32. What did Nyachom say when she was asked by her uncle?
33. What did Kulang do after the speech of Nyachom?
34. What did Kulang say after he was told that the girl was underage?
35. What do you think of the trick made by Kulang and Nyachom? Do you think Nyalora would be happy with her sister?
36. How would you advise the current generation in a case like this?

Chapter 2

1. What is the name of the family of Kulang's second wife?
2. What was the in-laws' answer when Kulang decided to marry their daughter?
3. How many days did Kulang give them to come back and what did he do after four days?
4. How did Kulang feel when he was not given wine? Who did he call?
5. Why did Kulang call Nyachom 'sister'?
6. After some days, Kulang came back to his in-laws for an emergency meeting. What was the agenda about? Why?
7. What accusations did Kulang level against the dogs?

8. What was his in-laws' answer?
9. What happened when Kulang saw one of his in-laws' dogs close to his house?
10. How did his in-laws discover the truth of Kulang's anger?
11. What did they do and how did Kulang feel at last?
12. How did Kulang retaliate against his in-laws?

Chapter 3
1. What was Kulang doing when his two brothers' in-law arrived in his house?
2. What did they bring with them to visit their sister's family?
3. What did Nyachom do in a hurry while her husband was absent? Why?
4. How long did it take for Kulang to arrive home?
5. How did Kulang feel and what question did he ask his in-laws?
6. How did his in-laws feel?
7. Kulang took his Thom in order to insult his in-laws with metaphor. What were the messages he said in Nuer language?
8. Why did the younger brother in-law leave on the same day?
9. What is the name of Kulang's elder brother in-law who remained with him?
10. Why didn't Kulang say 'good night' to Bilbor?
11. What news rocked the whole village in the morning?
12. Why did Bilbor decide to go to the war?
13. What happened to Bilbor at the battleground?
14. Which community was Bilbor fighting alongside?
15. Which community was Bilbor fighting against?
16. Which of the two communities lost the fight?
17. How did Kulang feel about Bilbor's death and what did he tell Nyachom when she was crying?

Chapter 4
1. Why did Kulang tell Jok Ruai Yut to take any vulture he recognized?
2. "May I taste the meat of your slaughtered cow." said the visitor. What was Kulang's answer?

3. What did Kulang say in the third question when he was asked by the visitor to direct him by showing him the way?
4. Assume you were in the place of the visitor Jok, what would you do or say?

Chapter 5
1. "I need the hippo's legs for I will give them to my uncle Golongpin."
a. Who said that?
b. To whom?
c. Where?
2. What did Gollongpin say when he received the two hippo's legs?
3. What orders did Kulang give his wife Nyachom when he received the hippo's legs?
4. What did Kulang's dog Ken-Thiäng-dak do to the hippo's legs when Nyachom was away?
5. When Nyachom knew that hippo's legs were eaten, what did she do before she could disclose the bad news to Kulang?
6. "Father of my kids, kill me." Nyachom told Kulang.
a. How did Kulang reply?
b. What did Kulang say when he finished eating the food which he thought was an appetizer?
7. "Your dog Ken-Thiäng-dak has eaten your hippo's legs." said Nyachom.
a. Why did Kulang pop out his eyes in shock?
b. What did Kulang say?
c. Why did Nyachom climb a tree?
d. Why did Kulang refuse the advice of Ruai Pab and the other guy?
e. What mechanism did Golongpin use to stop Kulang from killing his wife?
f. What was Kulang's reaction to Golongpin's advice?
8. Who came to Kulang's home when he slaughtered his goat?
9. What did he beg from Kulang?
10. How did Kulang reply the beggar and why did he cry?
11. How did the beggar insult Kulang when he knew Kulang would not give him any thing?
12. Was it right of Kulang to threaten his wife and to try to kill her?

Chapter 6
1. What did Kulang do with the wooden crutch of the sleeping crippled man?
2. What happened when the crippled man decided to go?
3. What question did the visitor ask Kulang when he found out that his crutch wasn't there?
4. What was Kulang's answer?
5. What did the crippled man decide after he knew that his crutch was intentionally burnt by Kulang?
6. Why did Kulang sell away his cow?

Chapter 7
1. Who was Kulang's close friend?
2. Why did Kulang want to end his companionship with him?
3. What failed mechanism did he use at first to separate them?
4. What did Kulang say about the moon's status?
5. What was Ruai Pab's input to the conversation which Kulang started?
6. How did Kulang successfully bring into an end their companionship with Ruai Pab?
7. Do you think losing a friend is worth it?

Chapter 8
1. What is the name of Kulang's first born child? What does it mean?
2. Why did Kulang call his son for a meeting?
3. What did Kulang tell his son when he first came with four youth?
4. What did Kulang tell his son again when he came with six youth?
5. What happened at last when Chamkuan brought twelve youth home with him?
6. Why did Kulang say Chamkuan's group had no lead singer?
7. How did Nyachom and Chamkuan feel when they were put to shame?

Chapter 9
1. What is the name of Kulang's nephew who brought sugar?
2. How did Pel put the sugar into the drinking pot of Kulang?

3. What did Kulang do with the sugar-water when he tried to mouth rinse?
4. Why did Kulang smile at his wife Nyachom?
5. Was Nyachom aware of the sugar being put into the water by Pel?
6. Why did Kulang lament and pour out the water that was given to him?
7. What warning did Kulang give Nyachom concerning the water?
8. How did Pel rescue Nyachom from Kulang's hand?
9. "Queen Nyachom, mother of my kids, where did you get it again, please?"
a. Who said that?
b. Why?
10. Why did Kulang give his cow to be sold out by Pel?
11. Why did Kulang call an emergency meeting with the villagers and his family?
12. What did Kulang do with four sack of sugar bought with the sold-out cow?
13. What did Kulang try to do in the morning and how did he feel?
14. How did Pel sympathize with his uncle?

Chapter 10
1. Recount the important messages brought to Kulang by the following kids?
a. What was the first kid's message?
b. What was the second kid's message?
c. What was the third kid's message?
d. What was the fourth kid's message?
2. How did Kulang feel when he received the messages?
3. How did Kulang try to move to all the places at the same time?
4. How did Nyachom help him?
5. Which place did Kulang visit first and why?
6. Which place did Kulang visit last?
7. What did Kulang say when he became tremendously satisfied?

Chapter 11
1. How many young men came to take Kulang's Loth? Did they succeed?
2. Why did Machar Tot visit Kulang's home?

3. What help did Machar give Kulang upon arriving?
4. How did Kulang feel?
5. What did Machar Tot ask at last?
6. Why did Kulang give away to Machar his expensive Loth?
7. What do you think would have happened if Machar Tot had eaten with Kulang?
8. Why is Bol Phal Muang mentioned in this part?

Chapter 12
1. What is the pet name of Gatkuoth Ruei Wuor?
2. Why did Kulang ask him a lot of impractical questions?
3. How many days did Gatkuoth spend in the house of Kulang?
4. What did Gatkuoth decide to do when he reached his home?
5. Who accompanied Gatkuoth to the home of Kulnag?
6. What time did they arrive in the house of Kulang?
7. What did Kulang angrily say when Gatkuoth asked for some drinking water?
8. Why did Gatkuoth eat alone and what was Kulang's sentiment?
9. Why did Kulang ask a lot of superior questions?
10. What happened to Kulang's saliva at last?
11. What did Kulang say when he was allowed to eat?
12. How did Gatkuoth affront him?
13. Why did Kulang apologize and what did he promise not to do again?

Chapter 13
1. How many Anyanya soldiers arrived at Kulang's home?
2. Who was in charge of the soldiers and who was their overall commander?
3. Why did Kulang become poignant and irritated when he saw them?
4. "Can your greeting be eaten?"
   a. Who said that?
   b. To whom?
c. Why?
5. What did Kulang tell the officer in charge?

6. How did the officer help Kulang?
7. What was Kulang's reaction?
8. When was Toch town opened?
9. What was Toch's name before?
10. Who commanded the soldiers to Kulang's home?
11. What did the soldiers do and what did Kulang tell them?
12. What does Longteem mean?

Chapter 14
1. Why did the boy run to Kulang's *Luak*?
2. What did Kulang tell him?
3. What was the boy's reaction?
4. What would you have done if you had been in the boy's place?

Chapter 15
1. Why did the police authority decide to bring Nyachom?
2. What mechanism did they use in order for Nyachom to come?
3. What did Kulang say about the Phone?

Chapter 16
1. Why was Kulang uninterested to greet his nephew?
2. How did Kulang's nephew know that his uncle didn't like him?
3. Did Kulang's nephew eat with him?
4. How did Kulang's nephew feel at the end?

Chapter 17
1. Why was Kulang monitoring the food?
2. Who was cooking the food?
3. What warning did Kulang give Nyachom regarding the danger?
4. Did Nyachom ignore her husband's warning?
5. Why did Kulang think that he was betrayed by Nyachom?
6. How did Nyachom restore back Kulang's happiness?

Chapter 18
1. As Nyachom was taking food to Kulang, what did her husband see from far?
2. What did the man from far put in his head?
3. Why did Kulang and Nyachom debate on the man from afar?
4. What was Kulang's/Nyachom's position on the debate?
5. What happened to the human figure from far at last?

Chapter 19
1. What was the traveler carrying?
2. What did the traveller give Kulang?
3. What was Kulang's wish when he tasted the dates?
4. How did Kulang blame God?
5. Which town did Kulang finally decide to visit? Why?
6. Where did he sit when he arrived in Dongola? Why?
7. Where can we find Dongola?

Chapter 20
1. What type of goat did the soldiers select?
2. What was Kulang's recommendation?
3. What trick did Kulang tell the soldiers concerning goat?
4. Which of the goats did the soldiers take?
5. Where did Kulang take the goat?
6. Why did he say he had rebelled?
7. How did he insult the soldiers in his rebellion declaration message?

Chapter 21
1. What is the name of Kulang's second dog?
2. What did the dog do that infuriated Kulang?
3. How did Kulang insult the dog?
4. What happened to Kulang while holding the food?

Chapter 22
1. What did the youngster find in front of Kulang?
2. What did Kulang tell him before they could eat/chat?
3. What did the youngster promise him?
4. What unbearable accusation did Kulang level against the youngster?
5. What was the youngster's reply?
6. Who insisted on the death accusation trick?
7. What did Kulang tell the boy at last?
8. What would have happened if the youngster had admitted the death accusation?
9. Do you think they would have eaten together even if he had accepted the death accusation?

Chapter 23
1. Who did Kulang see on his journey?
2. Why did Kulang get surprised?
3. What did Kulang tell the villagers when he returned?
4. What was Kulang expecting from his listeners?

Chapter 24
1. Who did Kulang send for?
2. What did Kulang's brother in-law bring?
3. When did Kulang become angry with his in-law?
4. How did Kulang approach his in-law?
5. How did Kulang's in-law reply him?

Chapter 25
1. How long did the flood last?
2. What did Kulang decide when the village was controlled by water?
3. Who divided the cattle with Kulang?
4. What did Kulang do with his part?
5. What happened at the end of the flood to Chamkuan's cattle?
6. What did Kulang do at the end of the flood?
7. What is the moral lesson of this story?
8. Should Kulang have explained his idea to Chamkuan?

Chapter 26
1. What kind of flood had Sudan experienced in 1966?
2. How did the youth do fishing?
3. What was the name of Kulang's child who went fishing?
4. What does the term 'Buttock' meant?
5. Who was harpooning with Duer?
6. How was Duer hit by the harpoon?
7. How did Duer take home the fish?

Chapter 27
1. What are the sources of livelihood across the Nuer-land?
2. What did Kulang do in 1950?
3. How many area units did Kulang label?
4. How did Kulang divide his eight area units for agriculture?
5. What happened to the crops after the heavy rain?
6. What happened in the land after short time?
7. How did Kulang advise the people who were complaining?
8. What does feddan mean?

Chapter 28
1. Where was Kulang when five young men arrived?
2. Where did the young men sit?
3. Who served the youth with water?
4. How were the young men smoking?
5. What did Kulang do when he noticed the presence of the people in his *Luak*?
6. How did the young men suffer?
7. How did Kulang accuse the young men?
8. How did Kulang leave the young men?
9. How did the young men regret?

Chapter 29
1. What were the soldiers doing when Kulang arrived?
2. How did Kulang interrupt the soldiers?

3. How did the soldiers reply?
4. What was Kulang's reaction when there was no salt?
5. Where did Kulang sit when he could not find the salt?
6. What did Kulang see when he was sitting?
7. What did Kulang do to the dog?
8. How did Kulang tactically insult the soldiers who refused to give him salt?

Chapter 30
1. Why did Kulang and Nyachom go to the river?
2. Who came to Kulang's family while in the river?
3. What did the soldiers see and fight over?
4. How did Kulang employ tactfulness?
5. What happened to Kulang's salt at last?
6. What is the moral lesson of the story?

Chapter 31
1. What don't the parents-in-law do at their daughter's home?
2. Who visited Nyachom during the daytime?
3. Where was Kulang when Nyachom's mother arrived?
4. Who served the mother in-law with food?
5. How did Kulang send a warning message for his mother in-law's continuous visits?
6. Was this a fair way for the mother in-law to be treated?
7. How would Nyachom feel about not being able to see her mother?

Chapter 32
1. What did Kulang put in the fire?
2. What did Kulang slap many times and why?
3. What did the bride want to talk about?
4. How did Kulang approach the bride?
5. What happened to Kulang's cucumber?
6. Where did the bride get fire from?

Chapter 33
1. Who took Kulang to the Church?
2. How did Kulang feel in the Church?
3. What drink was Kulang given?
4. What did Kulang say after the drinks?

Chapter 34
1. Who won the communal elections?
2. What did Kulang say about the winner?
3. Who was sued in court by Kulang?
4. How did the Head Chief help Kulang?

Chapter 35
1. Who did Kulang visit?
2. How was Kulang welcomed?
3. What was Kulang's agenda?
4. How did the man reply Kulang?
5. Who died between the two, Kulang and Tut?

Chapter 36
1. Where was Nyachom when Kulang left home?
2. What did Nyachom decide at home?
3. How did Nyachom approach Kulang among the crowd?
4. How did Kulang respond to Nyachom's approach?

Chapter 37
1. How many times did Kulang greet the deaf man?
2. Who did Kulang ask afterward?
3. What was Kulang told by the women?
4. What did Kulang tell the women at last?

Chapter 38
1. What did Kulang say when it rained?
2. How many people did Kulang praise to eat in the rainy day?
3. Why did Kulang mention some names?

Chapter 39
1. How long did the people suffer from the flood?
2. Where did Kulang and his kids go?
3. How did Kulang and his family enjoy and suffer at the same time in the river?
4. Why did Nyachom cry when they were about to reach home?
5. How did Kulang describe the river when he returned back home?

Chapter 40
1. Why did Kulang want Nyachom dead?
2. What tricks did Kulang use to notify Nyachom?
3. What did he try to do when there was no food cooked?
4. How did Nyachom survive the Kulang's death threat?
5. Should Kulang have threatened Nyachom with death?
6. What would you do if this happened to you?

Chapter 41
1. Who was a trickster?
2. How did the trickster befriend Kulang?
3. What did the trickster give to Kulang?
4. What did Kulang do to the gifts?
5. What did the trickster request from Kulang?
6. How did Kulang punish the man?
7. What was the man's alias or other name?
8. Who won the court judgement between the two friends, Kulang and Dhuorwia?
9. Where did the man go finally?

Chapter 42
1. What did Kulang do after a hot debate with Nyachom?
2. What did Nyachom tell her daughter before she could go?
3. Was Kulang listening to the conversation between Nyachom and her daughter?
4. What did Kulang say when Nyachom was talking to her daughter?

5. How did Nyachom reply?
6. What did Kulang say at last?
7. How did Kulang's and Nyachom's relation return to normalcy?
8. Should Nyachom have left?
9. Should Kulang have told Nyachom to go?
10. Would you want this to happen to you?

Chapter 43
1. Who arrived with kids at Kulang's home?
2. How did Kulang feel with the visitors?
3. How many children did arrive with their mother?
4. Which tactic did Kulang use to chase his sister in-law away?
5. What did Nyachom tell her sister when they reached home from the garden?
6. How did Kulang feel afterwards?
7. Should Kulang have threatened to kill his sister in-law?
8. How would Nyachom have felt about not being able to see her sister?
9. Is this how someone should behave nowadays?

Chapter 44
1. Who came in the morning to Kulang's home?
2. What was the agenda of the men's visit?
3. What did Kulang tell the men at first before Nyachom was called?
4. What was the dream's message about?
5. How did Kulang respond to the dream?
6. What demands did Kulang put in place before marrying the dead?
7. How did Kulang manage to chase the visitors away at last?
8. What did Nyachom do when she knew the men had gone?
9. Is 'Ghost Marriage' right to be continued in the Nuer community?
10. What are the advantages and disadvantages of the Ghost marriage?

Chapter 45
1. Who went for a journey with Kulang?
2. How did Kulang's family feel on the long journey?

3. What did Kulang's family decide to do on the way?
4. What were Kulang and kids given in the home on the way?
5. How did Kulang tell his children the habit of eating the food?
6. What happened to the food at last?
7. Was this the right thing to do?
8. Was Kulang being a good father to his kids?
9. How do you think Nyachom felt?
10. How do you think his kids felt?

Chapter 46
1. What did Kulang promise not to do again?
2. How did Nyachom reply to Kulang's demand?
3. How did Kulang convince Nyachom to stop eating food for life?
4. Why did Kulang regret his decision in the evening?

Chapter 47
1. What did Nyachom want to do in Kulang's hut?
2. How did Nyachom approach Kulang in cleaning the hut?
3. What demands did Kulang put in place?
4. How was Kulang's demand addressed by Nyachom?
5. What message did Kulang leave behind?

Chapter 48
1. What triggered the youth to fight against their neighbouring clan?
2. What did Kulang tell them when they were grouping?
3. Why didn't the youth accept Kulang's advice?
4. How did the fight end?
5. Whose clan lost the fight and whose clan lost a person?
6. What did Kulang tell the youth when they returned?
7. Why did Kulang want the cattle to lead the war?
8. What do you think on Kulang's decision?
9. What is a 'just war' according to Kulang?

Chapter 49
1. Why did Kulang's neighbour fail to plant his garden? How did he insult his neighbour?
2. How did Kulang help his neighbour?
3. Why did Kulang help his neighbour?
4. What happened to the wife of the neighbour?
5. What did she decide to do after she recovered? Why didn't Kulang tell her that he planted the garden?
6. Why did Kulang become happy at harvest time?

Chapter 50
1. When did Kulang die? How old was he when he died?
2. Who surrounded Kulang in his death-mat?
3. What are the good messages did Kulang leave behind?

Chapter 51
1. When did Nyachom die?
2. Who did Nyachom call to her death-mat?
3. What are the good messages did Nyachom leave behind?

A Glossary of Nuer Words and Phrases

Anyanya The Anyanya movement was the first Sudanese Civil War between the Africans of the country's southern part against the northern Arab-led government. Anyanya is a term in the Madi language which literally means 'snake venom'

Aywa Approval or to respond with agreement like 'Yes'.

Balang A young man who knows how to sing well and how to draw the attention of females. His songs are liked by all though he may not be handsome

Bier Dotted patterns on the face, culturally used as decoration.

Buur A place for cooking or a hearth with three earthen built stones to support the pot

Chi nhial deem kore-way-way
  A kids' song sung during the rain

Chotnyanga The hornless and grey ox

Chuolwich A person who died and whose body was not found as a result of a thunderstorm who is believed to safeguard people's lives against dangers when called

Dayiemni Small gods that advise and help the senior god

Ding-ding The sound of Kulang's Thom

Deng-Taath God of creation

Dhor-nyimaar-mi-ci-loch-tol-ehook-kama-wini
  Kulang's lamentation in anger or joy

Dow-nyaang Crocodile's child or the young one

Feddan(s) An agricultural unit(s) derived from an Arabic origin

Gaar Forehead marks or initiation into adulthood

Gare Lad

Gat- Prefix for a male name

Gat-Chiek Son of a woman (usually used as an insult)

Gat-guur Fellow or father's child (Nuer slang)

Gat-maar Brother

Gat-nyieri Nephew (especially sister's son)

Gatdila A real son of the land

Gatgualen	Cousin (especially on the father's side)
Geet-hook	Cattle thieves
Gen	A traditionally made papyrus bed high in the middle of the Luak with the fire bank underneath it
Guadinda	A term of respect for the elderly
Guan-gan	A term only used by women for their husbands or the father of their kids
Kachilooj	An interjection used to start a fight
Kaway	A white man
Koat	A tamarind tree
Kot	A traditional fan made of sisal leaves
Kop	A traditional dish
Kraal	A manger, stable or dwelling for cows
Kuar	The leader/boss
Kuoth	Almighty God
Kuuth/Kuoth	Gods/god
Kuoth-nhial	Heavenly God
Kuoth	
Kuoth kunen	God/God see this!
Kueny-goor	A stool for the elderly
Lalob tree	Balanites agyptiaca which is believed to be a member of either Zygophyllaceae or the Balanitaceae and grows in South Sudan
Leet/Let	Beasts/beast or wild animals that feed on human flesh
Lek	A type of catfish
Liach	A pregnant cow
Lieth	Butter
Lieth-yang	Sweet (butter) oil from the cow's milk Loth An ox's bell
Luak	The main compound or hut in which a family lives
Maa/Maath	Mr/Mister
Maale	A greeting of 'Is peace with you?' If ever you are greeted 'Maale' you can respond back 'Maale Mi diit or Maale Mi goa' which means: 'Great Peace or Peace for all.'
Naath	Another name for the Nuer tribe

Ngoth-ka-baaw
         An insult
Nok   A bird's feather placed on the head as a decoration
Nya-   A prefix name for a female that means 'daughter of –'
Nyabuobkah A traitor that retrieves and brings information
Nyame Miss/Mrs
Nyang   Crocodile
Pathoot A certain type of net used for fishing
Peeth   The evil eye
Piech   Another name for walwal
Pilual   An age group determined according to forehead marks
Rel-geng (wan)
         A fox
Shiekh   An Islamic word for the person leading the prayers in the mosque
Tamam   An Arabic expression which means 'good'
Tang-yoka A stick used in dancing
Thir-luak A tall tree branch used to support the Luak
Thom   A traditional musical instrument resembling a guitar
Thontuot A strong person
Tiach   Deep fried meat
Turuk   An intellectual person (derived from Turks)
Walwal   Light porridge (a common food for the Nuer tribe)
Walilili   Cheering shouts often heard during a fight.
O/oh/oy/ wa/ wo
         Indicate aw sound as in awful

Acknowledgments

Firstly, I would like to thank and appreciate Mr. Duoth Koang Ruei Wuor who, in 2001, wrote seventeen of Kulang's stories in the Nuer language, and who did not only permit me to write this book but also helped a lot in the collection of most of the stories.

Secondly, I do owe thanks and appreciations to the following individuals for their unwavering support in one way or another: Oyet Nathaniel, Gatwich Koang, Eng. William Garjang, Ustaz Peter Dador, Eng. Farouq Gatkuoth, Kang JJ, Michael Banychieng, Wek Paul, Gach Wan, Gatdeni Wugok, Naiem Mubarak, Luke Gatmai, Kim J. Liah, Dr. Hoth Giw, Puok Kamler, Matai Manuoi, Samuel Chuol, and Yohanis Musa.

I also wish to pay a profound tribute to Peter Deng and the entire staff of Africa World Books Pty Limited for believing in this book.

Finally, and above all, I thank God 'Kuoth-Nhial' that this book has solidly materialized.

I apologize for those whom I might have unintentionally omitted. They deserve my recognition and gratitude for the role they played in creating this book.

Weirial Gatyiel Puok Baluang
October, 2020

www.ingramcontent.com/pod-product-compliance
Lightning Source LLC
Chambersburg PA
CBHW032030290426
44110CB00012B/745